THE WILES LECTURES GIVE
THE QUEEN'S UNIVERSITY OF

CW00501556

The Swedish Imperial Experience
1560–1718

The Swedish Imperial Experience
1560–1718

MICHAEL ROBERTS

CAMBRIDGE UNIVERSITY PRESS

CAMBRIDGE

LONDON   NEW YORK   MELBOURNE

Published by the Syndics of the Cambridge University Press
The Pitt Building, Trumpington Street, Cambridge CB2 IRP
Bentley House, 200 Euston Road, London NW1 2DB
32 East 57th Street, New York, NY 10022, USA
296 Beaconsfield Parade, Middle Park, Melbourne 3206, Australia

First published 1979

Printed in Great Britain at the
University Press, Cambridge

Library of Congress Cataloguing in Publication Data

Roberts, Michael, 1908–

The Swedish imperial experience, 1560–1718.

(The Wiles lectures; 1977)

1. Sweden – History – 1523–1718 – Addresses, essays,
lectures. I. Title. II. Series.

DL 701.R63   948.5'02   78-58799

ISBN 0 521 22502 7

Contents

Maps

Preface

TO RECEIVE AN INVITATION to deliver the Wiles Lectures is an honour which in the course of the last twenty years has come to be greatly prized by historians; and though it must for the lecturer be a somewhat unnerving occasion, as he confronts those experts in his own field whom the University has invited from elsewhere to do battle with him, the warmth of the hospitality of the Department of Modern History ensures that it shall also be a pleasure. For me it was especially so, since it afforded me the opportunity to return to my old University; to renew contacts with old friends and colleagues, in and out of the Department; and not least to meet once more Mrs Janet Boyd, to whose munificent vision the Wiles Lectures owe their foundation and a great part of their characteristic flavour. To her, to Professor Lewis Warren, to the members of the Department, and to those who came from other universities to grace the occasion and by their contributions to the discussions to set right much (though I fear not all) that was amiss, I offer my sincere thanks.

Among the purposes which Mrs Boyd had in mind when the Lectures were first founded was that they should provide a historian with an opportunity to look back on his work, in the hope that he might be able to see it in broader perspective, and make his conclusions available to a rather wider and less specialized academic public. It was with this in mind that I pitched upon the topic of these lectures; though indeed I was perhaps hardly competent to pitch on any other. It was clearly impossible to include, in the space of four one-hour instalments, all that is here printed. In fact the book was written first, and the lectures were an attempt to convey the essence of it within the prescribed limits. It is hoped that despite the absence of a formal bibliography the footnotes may provide adequate indication of the authorities upon which I have relied; and by design the book is intended to be not so much an original contribution to knowledge as a reflection upon such knowledge as was already available to me: in which connexion it may be pertinent to add that the text was completed in December 1976.

M.R.

July 1977

for
Janet Boyd

SWEDEN - FINLAND, 1560

NORWAY

FINLAND

SWEDEN

Ladoga

Öregrund   Åbo
Åland   Helsingfors
Uppsala   INGRIA
Västerås   Narva
Stockholm   Reval
                  ESTONIA
Dago   Gdov
Norrköping   Osel   Dorpat
Söderköping   RUSSIA
Älvsborg   Pskov
Jönköping   LIVONIA
SMÅLAND   Gotland
            Öland   Windau   Riga
DENMARK   KURLAND   Düna
Copenhagen   Libau   Düna
  Lund
  Malmö   Memel   LITHUANIA
Bornholm   Njemen
Stralsund   Danzig   Königsberg
Stettin   PRUSSIA

BALTIC SEA

WHITE SEA

0   100   200   300   400
KILOMETRES

I

The Making of the Empire

THE SIXTEENTH AND SEVENTEENTH CENTURIES saw the foundation of those great modern empires in whose liquidation it has been our dubious destiny to acquiesce: the empires of Portugal, of Spain, of the Dutch, of England, and of France. Two of them, at all events – those of the Dutch and of Portugal – were based on small countries, neither of which had hitherto shown any likelihood of emerging as a great power, and they must always appear astonishing outbursts of energy: in the long view, perhaps, historical aberrations which Time must sooner or later rectify. But whether aberrations or no, they were, for good or ill, such remarkable records of human achievement, and set so deep an impress on vast areas of the world, that they must remain of perennial interest to the historian, troubling the ocean of history like those unpredictable freak waves which make the seas breasted by their caravels so formidable to mariners.

But the sixteenth and seventeenth centuries provided another example of imperial expansion, which at first sight must appear equally improbable; and which did indeed astonish contemporaries: the empire which Sweden made for herself in the Baltic, and in Germany, in the century between 1560 and 1660. And it is that empire which I hope to analyse in these lectures. For the most part it was acquired at break-neck speed: less than forty years separates the capture of Riga (1621) and the peace of Oliva. Its disintegration was equally swift: it may be said to have begun in 1702, when Peter the Great took Nöteborg (the future Schlüsselburg); and it was virtually complete when, sixteen years later, the bullet of an enemy (or possibly of a patriot) put an end to Charles XII's existence. Upon the history of mankind it left no permanent mark; and even upon the territories which were included in it exercised an influence which was for the most part transient. But in its day it was a tremendous fact; and to later

I

historians it is a fascinating challenge. Hitherto, there has been no single study, apart from one necessarily brief essay by Sven Lundkvist, which attempts an assessment of the whole experience. So, though in the long perspectives of history it may appear as no more than a ripple in a back-water, yet I make no apology for considering it.

How are we to account for this eccentric political phenomenon? Why did this highly unlikely development occur? What forces lay behind it, what peculiar circumstances, at home and abroad, permitted, facilitated, or perhaps compelled it? What was the nature of the empire which resulted, what the effects of the imperial experience on the conqueror and on the conquered? And why did the phenomenon prove so transient, the structure so fragile, the collapse so rapid and so total? These are some of the questions which I have put to myself, and to some of which, though not quite to all, I hope to provide at least some sort of an answer.

It seems clear, in the first place, that the Swedish empire was of a very different nature and provenance from those other empires which were contemporary with it. Those empires can all, perhaps, be described as empires of enterprise, of exploitation, of opportunity: perhaps even to some extent as empires of accident. Lying as they did at immense distances, sundered from the motherland by months of ocean voyaging, not one of them had direct strategic relevance to the metropole; though the rivalry of Dutch and Portuguese in Brazil or Indonesia might indeed centre on control of locally important strategic positions, and though such control might certainly have great economic significance for the colonial power. The Swedish empire, on the contrary, was an essential element in Sweden's defences. It is clear, too, that the Swedish expansion differed radically from the others in that it was not a more or less spontaneous outburst of the national energies, endogenously generated by forces which remain obscure: it was essentially a response to challenges from the outside. It may have been an empire of necessity; but by no stretch of imagination could it be described as an empire acquired by accident. It was the creation of deliberate policy, in that each addition to it was seen as necessary, and was the result of state action: private enterprise had no part in it. There was no place here for great proconsuls or wealthy corporations.

What, then, was the dynamic behind the Swedish expansion? It is a question to which more than one answer is available: as so often in Swedish historiography, there is an old school of thought and a new, and they come to widely differing conclusions. It fortunately happens that the available literature in English on the whole clearly reflects the views of the Old School; and this, perhaps, may serve to relieve me of the need to do more than remind you of the general run of their arguments.

The Old School, then, contended that the Swedish empire was essentially a reaction to, and the product of, past history: first to the struggle for national independence from Denmark; secondly, and more potently, to great international upheavals which were not of Swedish origin at all, and which were beyond Swedish control: the consolidation and outward thrust of the Muscovite state; the disintegration of the Baltic *status quo* in the mid-sixteenth century as a result of the decline of the Hanse and the collapse of the old Crusading Order of the Livonian Knights – itself in part a side-effect of the Reformation; and lastly, the international repercussions of the Counter-Reformation. All these developments, it is argued, directly affected Sweden's safety. Thus the real dynamic behind the creation of the empire was simply fear; and its initial objective, security. In this it contrasted absolutely with other contemporary empires, for whom the question of security – and by this I mean security of the metropole – had no part in the process of empire-building. It may be granted that absolute security is a chimaera; and the pursuit of it is apt to exercise an addictive effect upon those statesmen who devote themselves to it. And it cannot be denied that the search for security at times led Swedish statesmen to seek it in very strange places: in Alsace, at Olmütz, on the Brenner, in Kraków. It led them, too, to a far-flung diplomacy which at times embraced the Tatars of the Crimea, the Patriarch of Constantinople, the Zaporozhian Cossacks, the princes of Transylvania and Moldavia, and a motley collection of rebels against their lawful sovereigns. These diplomatic extravagances were invariably disappointing, occasionally disastrous, and not seldom farcical. But the excesses and exaggerations of the search for security must not blind us to the possibility that the search was justified. The historians of the Old School insisted that throughout the whole century and a half of her imperial career, Sweden found herself hemmed in between two hostile powers: on the one hand Denmark, anxious to reverse the verdict of 1523 and once more unite Scandinavia under a single sovereign – or, if that proved impossible, to keep Sweden in a permanent condition of military and economic weakness; on the other hand the emergent Muscovite state, with its ambitions to expand towards the Gulf of Bothnia, into the Scandinavian Arctic, and above all towards the Gulf of Finland and the Estonian coast. Successive kings of Sweden reacted to the situation by pre-emptive strikes, anxious aggressions, swift exploitation of opportunities which might well prove transient, in the hope thereby of buttressing their defences or deepening the protective zones which surrounded them.

Their apprehensions were the consequence of the hard facts of geography and the unforgotten lessons of recent history. A glance at the map will make clear the lines of force directed against the Swedish state. Denmark was in a position to close the Sound to Swedish trade: she could cut Sweden off from western markets and Atlantic salt; she threatened Sweden's solitary window to the open sea, at Älvsborg. From the Great Belt to the Gulf of Riga her islands stretched like a great boom across the Baltic, and were the warrant for her pretension to lordship of the sea; from her provinces north of the Sound, from the associated kingdom of Norway, her kings were able to launch attacks which might threaten Sweden's very existence. Twice between 1560 and 1613 such an attempt was made; and though each time it was beaten off, the cost of survival was high. For on each occasion the Danes captured Älvsborg; and on each occasion Älvsborg had to be bought back by war-indemnities of crushing severity. The memory of these experiences did not fade: when in 1643 Torstensson marched his army into Jutland, men said in Sweden that he was going to find out what had become of Älvsborg's ransom. Swedish propaganda did not fail to point out, as a warning example to patriots,[1] that Norway had lost her ancient independence and become a vassal-kingdom of the Danish crown. And Swedish statesmen were always prone to persuade themselves (on very slender evidence) that the Norwegians would embrace any suitable opportunity to throw off the Danish yoke: Charles X in

---

[1] E.g. in Gustav Adolf's speech at the opening of the riksdag of 1625: C. G. Styffe, *Konung Gustaf II Adolfs skrifter* (Stockholm 1861), pp. 214–17.

THE THREAT FROM
DENMARK, 1560 - 1645

WHITE
SEA

NORWAY

S W E D E N

F I N L A N D

Ladoga

Kopparberget O

Gävle

Öregrund

Åbo

Åland

Helsingfors

INGRIA

Sala O

Uppsala

Narva

Vuoksu

Västerås O

Vaxholm

Reval

ESTONIA

BOHUSLÄN

Läckö

Stockholm

Dagö

Hapsal

RUSSIA

Skara

O Norrköping

Ösel

Visingsborg

Vadstena

LIVONIA

Älvsborg

Göteborg

B A L T I C

Jönköping

Visby

Gotland

Windau

KURLAND

Duna

HALLAND

S E A

Kalmar

Öland

Libau

Duna

DENMARK

Copenhagen

BLEKINGE

Lund

Malmö

LITHUANIA

Bornholm

Njemen

PRUSSIA

0   100   200   300   400
KILOMETRES

SWEDISH GAINS FROM DENMARK

at Brömsebro 1645

at Copenhagen 1660

NORWAY

JÄMTLAND

HÄRJEDALEN

SWEDEN

FINLAND

WHITE SEA

Kopparberget O

Uppsala O

Ladoga

Västerås O

INGRIA

Stockholm

Åland

ESTONIA

BOHUSLÄN

Läckö O O Mariestad

Dagö

Älvsborg O O Göteborg

Ösel

LIVONIA

RUSSIA

Gotland

BALTIC SEA

KURLAND

Duna

Öland

DENMARK

BLEKINGE

Copenhagen

Lund

Malmö

Bornholm

LITHUANIA

Njemen

Duna

PRUSSIA

0   100   200   300   400

KILOMETRES

1659, Charles XI in 1678, Charles XII in the last two years of his life (to say nothing of Gustav III), all dreamed of a quick conquest and painless incorporation of Norway.

No doubt it is true that after 1624[1] it must have been increasingly clear that the danger of subjection by Denmark had ceased to be a reality. No doubt there came a moment in 1628 when circumstances forced the two countries into alliance for common defence against Habsburg. But by this time it had become an axiom of Swedish policy that Denmark was the unsleeping enemy. Axel Oxenstierna and Gustav Adolf each considered a preventive war against Denmark as a preliminary, or alternative, to the war in Germany;[2] in 1639 Oxenstierna told the Council that Denmark had 'repeatedly chucked us under the chin to see whether our teeth sat firm in our head';[3] and four years later the pre-emptive strike was duly carried out. The resulting peace of Brömsebro, by handing over Jämtland, Härjedalen and Halland to Sweden, began the process of giving Sweden her natural geographical limits. But the fear of Denmark remained; reinforced now by the possibility of a Danish *revanche*. That fear played its part in the choice of territorial gains which Sweden made at the peace of Westphalia: the acquisition of Bremen and Verden was welcomed as being (in Per Brahe's words) 'a stopper for the Jute'.[4] The idea of a preventive war against Denmark, while that country was still weak, was much in the minds of members of the Council when they debated the need for arming in December 1654.[5] Similar ideas, as it happened, were prevalent in Copenhagen: even in the early forties Denmark had felt herself encircled; and the Danish attack on Sweden in 1657 was dictated by anxiety not to let slip a possibly fleeting opportunity to obtain the security which they sought: as one Danish statesman put it, 'peace was more dangerous than war'.[6] And already the marriage

[1] When Gustav Adolf won a decisive diplomatic victory over Christian IV at the frontier conference at Sjöaryd.

[2] See, e.g. *Rikskansleren Axel Oxenstiernas skrifter och brevväxling* (*AOSB*) (1888–) I.vi.39–40; *Svenska riksrådets protokoll* (*RRP*) I.234–7.

[3] *RRP* VII.385 (17 January 1639).

[4] Yngve Lorents, *Efter Brömsebrofreden. Svenska och danska förbindelser med Frankrike och Holland 1645–1649* (Uppsala 1916), p. 100.

[5] *RRP* XVI.12.

[6] Finn Askgaard, *Kampen om Östersjön på Carl X Gustafs tid* (*Carl X Gustaf-Studier*) (Haderslev 1974), pp. 15, 99.

of Charles X had already inaugurated the fatal dynastic connexion with Holstein–Gottorp which turned that duchy into a Swedish puppet-state whose function was to threaten Denmark from the rear – much as France had tried to use Scotland in Tudor times – and so made normal relations with Denmark almost impossible. The logical conclusion of this anti-Danish policy was reached by Charles X, who launched his onslaught in 1658 with the avowed programme of annihilating Denmark as an independent state: the Danish royal family was to be imprisoned; the Danish aristocracy dispersed and deported; the city of Copenhagen was to be razed to the ground.[1] This programme, fortunately, proved beyond his powers; but when peace came in 1660 it brought to Sweden the rich province of Skåne, and so completed the process of attainment of natural boundaries which had been begun at Brömsebro.

This unsleeping fear of Denmark was not a political fantasy or an insubstantial nightmare. Until 1613 a Danish conquest was conceivable; until 1643 Danish encirclement was as much a reality as Swedish encirclement seemed to be to Christian IV; until 1721 a resounding Danish revenge, and the recovery of the provinces lost in 1645 and 1660, was at least a possibility. It was the fear of being imprisoned in the Baltic that led to Charles IX's provocative forward policy in Lappmark; it was the same fear which led Charles X to extort the cession of Trondheim at the peace of Roskilde in 1658. When in 1700 Denmark and Russia made their joint attack upon Sweden, Frederick IV was reaping the late harvest of more than sixty years of patient Danish diplomacy. And it is not to be forgotten that it had been fear of a Danish presence in Estonia, no less than of a Russian, which had led Eric XIV to take Reval under his protection, and so initiate the process which was to result in the creation of Sweden's transmarine empire. With Denmark established on Bornholm, Gotland, Ösel, no Swedish king (not even Gustav Vasa) could contemplate the re-establishment of the old Danish sphere of influence on the southern shore of the Gulf of Finland.

The prospect of war on two fronts – of being caught in a

[1] Lauritz Weibull, 'Från Kiel till Köbenhavn i augusti 1658', *Scandia* 1929, pp. 292–3, 311; *RRP* XVIII.87–8. Charles X feared that on grounds of convenience and accessibility Copenhagen might become the capital of any united Scandinavian state, and Sweden become no more than an appendage of Denmark: see Charles X to Biörenklou, 2 March 1658, in C. Adlersparre, *Historiska samlingar*, v (Stockholm 1822), p. 179.

pincer-movement between Denmark and Muscovy – had emerged long before the seventeenth century. Between the last quarter of the fifteenth century and the middle of the sixteenth the consolidated Muscovite realm for the first time flexed its youthful muscles and lunged outwards towards the sea. The collapse of the Livonian Knights in the 1550s gave Ivan IV the chance for which Russia had been waiting: in the vacuum of power thus left behind in Livonia, Russia, Poland and Denmark sought, with dubious titles but indubitable violence, to impose their dominion upon a ravaged and lordless land. A decisive moment came in 1558, when Ivan captured Narva, and thus for the first time gave Moscow free access to the sea.

The consequences of this event were far-reaching. The town of Reval, fearing the ruin of her trade and the loss of her middleman's profits, in 1560 offered to put herself under Swedish protection. Eric XIV accepted that offer; and by doing so laid the first stone of his country's Baltic empire. But the motive that prompted him (it is argued), was essentially precautionary: the necessity to make sure that no hostile or potentially hostile power should establish itself along the southern shore of the Gulf of Finland: not Denmark; and above all, not Russia. The fear of a Russian break-through to the Baltic was widespread in Europe,[1] and not least in Sweden. Already in Eric's time Swedish statesmen foresaw that the vastness of Russia, its limitless human resources, inherent strength and expansive force, would be the great danger they had to face in the future; and soon afterwards a spine-chilling prophecy became current, which predicted that in the year 1591 a Russian invasion of Finland would lead to the total destruction of the Swedish realm.[2] Already they had seen that they must either fight the Russians or be friends with them: successive generations would swing between these political alternatives.

In this view, then Sweden's lodgment in Estonia had as one of its objects the prevention of any irruption of the Muscovite to the Baltic shore; and thereafter the construction of an ever-deeper buffer-zone to insulate that lodgment from a Russian resurgence. For the foothold in Estonia could hardly be maintained if it were

[1] Georg von Rauch, 'Moskau und die europäischen Mächte des 17. Jahrhunderts', *Historische Zeitschrift (HZ)* 1954, p. 27.

[2] Kari Tarkiainen, 'Faran från öst i svensk säkerhetspolitisk diskussion inför Stolbovafreden', *Scandia* 1974, pp. 36–7.

bounded by the mediaeval walls of Reval. If Reval itself were to be safe it must be provided with some sort of hinterland, if only to deny to possible enemies the bases from which an attack could be mounted against it. But once the capture of neighbouring strongholds was begun, who could define the limits of strategic necessity, or set bounds to the process of expansion? The need for some sort of defence in depth appeared clearly in the time of John III, when the Swedes fought desperately, and for the most part alone, to stem the advance of the Muscovite to the sea. Not until the 1580s did the tide begin to turn in their favour. In 1581 Pontus de la Gardie took Narva. Its transference to Swedish control did indeed mark the end of its hectic prosperity; but it also marked the end of one of Ivan's most cherished commercial ambitions. When peace was made at Teusina in 1595, the whole of Estonia passed into Swedish hands. After a quarter of a century of war, Sweden found herself, not with an outpost, but with an overseas dominion.

Ten years later the threat from the east assumed a new character. Between 1605 and 1613 Russia was submerged in the anarchy of the Time of Troubles; and for a time it seemed possible that one solution to the confusion might lie in the election of a Polish Tsar. The consequences of such a union, at a time when Swedish and Polish forces were already fighting each other in Livonia, might be expected to be disastrous. In an effort to avert the danger Charles IX himself intervened in the Russian imbroglio; and Gustav Adolf after him put forward his brother as a candidate for the Muscovite throne. The attempt to give Russia a Swedish Tsar did indeed fail, though by a narrow margin; but the difficulties of Michael Romanov, struggling simultaneously against Polish and Swedish invasions, presented Sweden with a unique and fleeting opportunity to add a new defensive buttress in the east. Gustav Adolf did not fail to seize it. He was not, indeed, able to annex the vast areas of north-west Russia which had been included in his original peace-terms;[1] but the peace of Stolbova in 1617 for the first time gave to Sweden a deliberately-chosen strategic frontier.[2] By adding Ingria to the Swedish dominions it shut Russia off from the sea; it blocked Moscow's

[1] AOSB I.ii.246; M. Roberts, Gustavus Adolphus. A History of Sweden 1611–1632, I (London 1953), pp. 86–8.   [2] Tarkiainen, 'Faran från öst', pp. 44, 47.

THE THREAT FROM RUSSIA
AND SWEDISH GAINS

at Teusina 1595

at Stolbova 1617

WHITE
SEA

NORWAY

FINLAND

Vasa

KEXHOLMS
LÄN

SWEDEN

Kexholm   Ladoga

Gävle   Ladoga
Öregrund   Nyen   Stolbova
Uppsala   Åland   Åbo
                         Helsingfors
Vaxholm   INGRIA
Stockholm   Reval   Narva Teusina
                     Dagö   Jama
Norrköping   Hapsal ESTONIA Ivangorod
                     Ösel   Volchov
                              Pernau   Dörpat   Novgorod

                                         RUSSIA
                    Gotland
                 Windau   LIVONIA   Pskov

Kalmar Öland   Riga
                    Libau KURLAND Kirkholm
DENMARK   Düna

              Memel   Düna
Bornholm   LITHUANIA
                    Niemen
          Putzig
        Königsberg
Danzig

    PRUSSIA   0   100 200 300 400
                         KILOMETRES

BALTIC SEA

attempts to penetrate westward into the Scandinavian Arctic; in a word, it arrested Russia's territorial expansion into Europe for almost forty years. Gustav Adolf was perhaps the first European statesman to appreciate the potentialities of Russia within the European state-system: after Stolbova the maintenance of good relations with Moscow, on the basis of a common enmity to Poland, was one of the cardinal points of Swedish foreign policy throughout the whole period of the Thirty Years War, and Sweden was the first foreign country to maintain a permanent diplomatic representative in Moscow. The Russians were not insensible of these attentions, and fully appreciated the advantages of Swedish goodwill: they celebrated the victory of Breitenfeld, and mourned the fatal day of Lützen. At Westphalia Alexis was even referred to (incorrectly) as Sweden's ally.[1] Thus for nearly two generations the Russian peril slumbered: in the 1650s it was to awake again, never thereafter to be conjured away. Charles X's foreign policy had at least this merit, that it squarely faced that uncomfortable fact.[2]

It was thus (so the Old School argued) an intelligible and real fear of Russia which led to Sweden's expansion into Estonia, Ingria and Kexholm; just as it was an intelligible and real fear of Denmark which led ultimately to the incorporation of Bohuslän, Halland, Skåne and Blekinge. And the Polish war and the acquisition of Livonia were explained in similar terms. That war originated in the great dynastic quarrel within the Vasa family, which was provoked by the expulsion of King Sigismund from Sweden, and the usurpation of the younger Vasa line in the person of Charles IX. This violent proceeding was justified as a necessary defensive measure to safeguard Swedish Protestantism from the threat of an allegedly catholicizing monarch; but (like the English Revolution of 1689, to which it is in many respects analogous) it had much wider international implications. The dynastic quarrel became involved in the greater religious struggle which was moving to the disaster of the Thirty Years War. For two generations the rulers of Sweden feared the restoration by force

[1] von Rauch, 'Moskau und die europäischen Mächte', pp. 30, 31, 34.
[2] See Bohdan Kentrschynskyj, Karl X Gustaf inför krisen i öster (Stockholm 1956); id., 'Ukrainska revolutionen och Rysslands angrepp mot Sverige 1656', Scandia 1966; Birger Åsard, 'Upptakten till Karl X Gustafs anfall mot Polen 1655', Scandia 1970.

of arms of the elder, legitimate, line; much as the rulers of England were haunted by the threat from the Jacobites. After Gustav Adolf's death the succession was so precarious that Axel Oxenstierna did not hesitate to say that Sweden's real war was not with the Imperialists or the Catholic League, but with Poland.[1] It is probably true that the danger of a Polish restoration was exaggerated, that the prospects of a successful Polish invasion were poor, that the assumption that the return of the Polish Vasas would automatically lead to the recatholicization of Sweden was unwarranted.[2] But this was not a matter on which men reasoned calmly. The Polish Vasas refused to give up their claims; and that fact was enough to obstruct the conclusion of a lasting peace for some sixty years. Charles IX's intervention in Russia had been provoked by the fear that Sigismund or his son might succeed in securing the Russian throne, and so be in a position to encircle Estonia and take Finland and Sweden in the rear. And it was in an effort to force a peace (but also to deny Sigismund invasion-bases) that Sweden later put pressure on Poland by resuming the invasion of Polish territory. Hence the seizure of Riga in 1621, when Poland was preoccupied with a Turkish invasion; hence the over-running of Polish Livonia in the years that followed; hence the transference of the theatre of war to Polish Prussia in 1626, with the idea of blocking the export of Polish corn from the Vistula delta, in the hope that the *szlachta* would compel their king to come to terms. So Livonia became a Swedish province, though in the beginning there had been no intention of a permanent conquest; and a man could walk from Stockholm to Riga on Swedish soil. But it need not have been so: Gustav Adolf had been willing, in 1622 and 1623, to restore these conquests in return for a firm peace.[3]

Twenty years later, under the impact of Chmelnicki's revolt and

[1] *AOSB* I.xiii.27–9, where Oxenstierna writes to the Regents (7 January 1635): '[we should] keep both our eyes fixed on the Polish business, as being Y.M.'s private, direct concern, and let the German business be left to the Germans, who will be the only people to get any advantage out of it (if there is any); and therefore not expend any more men or money here, but rather try by all means to wriggle out of it, and apply all the country's resources to the Polish war.'

[2] As Mankell argued long ago: J. Mankell, *Om Gustaf II Adolfs politik* (Stockholm 1881), pp. 13–30

[3] *AOSB* II.i.200, Jonas Hallenberg, *Svea Rikes Historia under Konung Gustaf Adolf den Stores Regering* (Stockholm 1796), V, pp. 42–4.

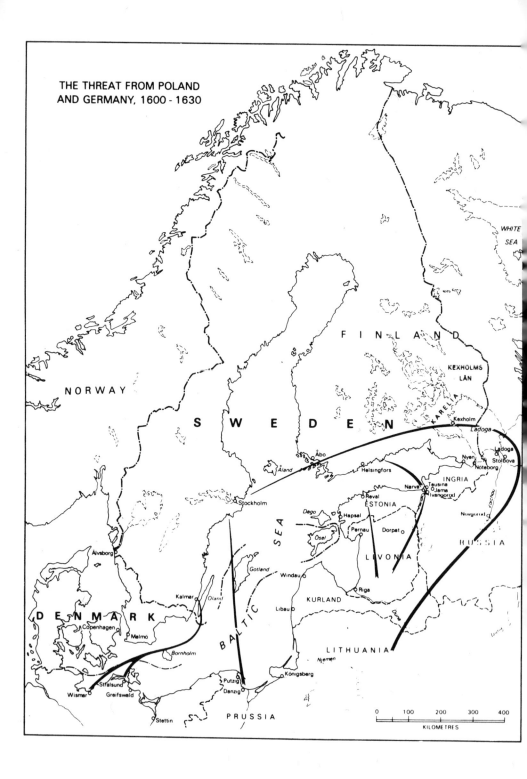

THE THREAT FROM POLAND
AND GERMANY, 1600 - 1630

WHITE
SEA

NORWAY

FINLAND

KEXHOLMS
LÄN

SWEDEN

KAREILA

Kexholm

Ladoga

Åbo

Ladoga

Helsingfors

Nyen

Storbova

Åland

Noteborg

INGRIA

Narva

Teusina

Stockholm

Jama

Ivangorod

Reval

ESTONIA

Novgorod

Dago

Hapsal

Osel

Pernau

Dorpat

RUSSIA

LIVONIA

Älvsborg

Gotland

Windau

Riga

Kalmar

Öland

KURLAND

DENMARK

Libau

Copenhagen

Malmö

Bornholm

LITHUANIA

BALTIC SEA

Njemen

Putzig

Königsberg

Stralsund

Danzig

Wismar

Greifswald

0   100   200   300   400

Stettin

PRUSSIA

KILOMETRES

Russian intervention, Poland seemed to be disintegrating; and for the first time since 1617 Sweden saw Russia reaching out for the Baltic ports, threatening to circumvent the buffer which Gustav Adolf had erected. To Charles X there appeared to be only two ways of meeting this danger: either an alliance with Poland to stop the Russians; or, if that were unattainable, immediate intervention against Poland to forestall the Russian onslaught.[1] The first alternative proved impossible to obtain, because the sacrifices he demanded of Poland in return for his assistance were too high. The other alternative was therefore pursued. It was essentially a repetition of the policy which Sweden had deployed against Russia in the years 1610–17, namely, to seize a transient opportunity to deepen and extend her security-zone in this area. So Charles X aimed at the subjection of Kurland, the occupation of Polish Prussia, and the control of ducal Prussia by compelling the Elector of Brandenburg to hold it as a fief of the Swedish crown.

Meanwhile, Sweden had expanded into Germany: it was the crucial development which transformed her from a merely Baltic to a European power. And, once again, the considerations which led to that fateful step were explained by historians of the Old School in terms of an essentially defensive operation, designed to meet dangers both political and religious. In some sort, of course, the German venture was a corollary, or sequel, to the struggle with Poland: Habsburg aid to Sigismund was one of the causes which Gustav Adolf adduced for intervention. But more broadly the establishment of a Habsburg domination was feared as portending a Universal Monarchy, an upsetting of the international order; while concern for the Evangelical Cause in Germany reflected the conviction that the fate of Protestantism everywhere was one and indivisible. In 1630 the Island World (to borrow Ludwig Dehio's term) intervened to restore the Precarious Balance, precisely at the moment when the Turks, who normally discharged that office, happened not to be available as a counterweight.[2] In the narrower context of Sweden's national interests, the consequences of an Imperial victory were expected

---

[1] A characteristic example of the point made by Georg Landberg, that war and alliance were not so much opposites in this period as alternatives: Georg Landberg, *Johan Gyllenstiernas nordiska förbundspolitik* (Uppsala 1935), pp. 14–44.

[2] See Ludwig Dehio, *The Precarious Balance* (London 1963), *passim*.

to be the establishment of a formidable and hostile power in the
north German Baltic ports, and the creation of a navy in those
ports which would imperil Sweden's quasi-insular security. The
harbours of Pomerania and Mecklenburg were to Sweden what
the Channel ports were to England.[1]

The fear of invasion, the concern to keep possible invasion-ports
out of the hands of enemies, reinforced a determination not to
permit the existence of a hostile fleet within the Baltic. This
determination found expression in the concept of *dominium maris
Baltici*. In its primary significance the doctrine meant no more than
the denial of the *use* of Baltic waters to hostile or potentially
hostile fleets, and implied no consequential claim to control of
Baltic coastlands; but in practice, as a simple matter of naval
strategy, the control of harbours was tacitly accepted as a
corollary. The phrase itself seems to date from the 1560s and to
have been coined by Sigismund II Augustus of Poland; though
it does not seem to have been used in an official document in
Sweden before 1614, when it appeared (ironically enough, in view
of later history) in Sweden's treaty of alliance with the Dutch.[2]
Sweden was not the only Baltic country to claim *dominium maris*:
despite the smouldering enmity between them, the two
Scandinavian powers were at least in agreement that the *jus classis
immitendae* was to be a Scandinavian monopoly. Certainly they
were not prepared to concede such a right to Poland: an article
of the treaty of Stuhmsdorf in 1635 forbade Poland to give naval
assistance to Sweden's enemies,[3] and the Swedish negotiators had
tried in vain to insert another forbidding the building of any Polish
fleet. By 1637, thanks to the efforts of Sigismund III and
Władysław IV, that fleet had become too powerful to be ignored.
Christian IV did not ignore it: the Danish navy put to sea, and

[1] To Sigmund Goetze, whose spirited revival of some of the contentions of
nineteenth-century Catholic historians represents a timely correction of the historio-
graphical balance, Swedish objectives would be better defined as the perpetuation of
German political weakness on the Baltic littoral, and the atomization of Germany under
the twin pretexts of religion and 'German liberties'. Sigmund Goetze, *Die Politik des
schwedischen Reichskanzlers Axel Oxenstiernas gegenüber Kaiser und Reich* (Kiel 1971),
especially pp. 45–51, 149, 170, 176, 214–18, 236–8, 243–4; *cf.* Curt Weibull, 'Gustaf
II Adolf', *Scandia* 1929, p. 21.
[2] Nils Ahnlund, 'Dominium maris baltici', in Ahnlund, *Tradition och historia*
(Stockholm 1956), pp. 115–30.
[3] *Sverges traktater med främmande magter*, v₂ (Stockholm 1909) (§xxi).

without a declaration of war destroyed it.[1] Any Polish efforts to recover from that blow were jealously watched: one of the arguments for Charles X's attack on Poland in 1655 was that the Poles were negotiating with the Dutch for naval assistance.[2] And as with Poland, so with other powers. It was one of the most important reasons for Gustav Adolf's exultation over the peace of Stolbova that it prevented the appearance of a Russian fleet in the Baltic. His propaganda contended that Habsburg moves to build a fleet in Wismar were a violation of a right which Sweden had enjoyed 'time out of mind', and the prohibition of any Habsburg navy was a major point in the demands which Sweden drew up for the congress in Danzig in 1630. It seems an over-simplification of a situation which had many aspects to write (as Sven Lundkvist does): 'Sweden's success in that war [*sc.* against Poland] entailed a corresponding revision of her objectives: by 1630 they had come to include a *dominium maris Baltici*. Intervention in the Thirty Years War now appeared as a logical corollary to what had gone before.'[3] The intervention could equally well be described as the logical corollary of an evangelical foreign policy stretching back to Charles IX's time: and the objectives were not 'revised' to include the doctrine of *dominium maris*: an already existing doctrine was simply applied to a new challenger of it. The 'Redemption Treaty' of 1649 between Denmark and the Dutch was particularly resented in Sweden as a violation of established convention, since it allowed the passage of an unlimited number of Dutch warships through the Sound.[4] When by the treaty of Labiau Sweden recognized the Great Elector as sovereign in East Prussia, care was taken to deny him the right to keep a navy.[5] The peace of Roskilde foundered on the article which

---

[1] In 1638 Christian IV put forward a claim, not only to *dominium maris Baltici*, but also to *dominium maris septentrionalis*, and this may have been one reason why Władysław IV attempted to introduce customs-dues at Danzig, in order to build up his navy: Sune Dalgård, 'Østersø, Vestersø, Nordsø. Dominium Maris Baltici og Maris Septentrionalis', [Dansk] *Historisk Tidsskrift*, 11 Raekke, Bd. 5 (1957), pp. 295–320.

[2] See Ehrensteen's Relation, printed in *Sveriges riddderskaps och adels riksdagsprotokoll* (*SRARP*) VII.114, 139; and Åke Lindquist, 'Svenskarna och De Byes beskickningar 1654–1655', *Karolinska Förbundets Årsbok* (*KFÅ*) 1941, pp. 9–10, 16–19.

[3] Sven Lundkvist, 'The Experience of Empire', in *Sweden's Age of Greatness*, ed. M. Roberts (London 1973), p. 31.

[4] Askgaard, *Kampen om Östersjön*, p. 17. This concession was revoked by the 'Rescission Treaty' of 26 September 1653.

[5] Birger Fahlborg, *Sveriges yttre politik 1660–1664* (Stockholm 1932), p. 31.

concerned the barring of foreign fleets. And when in 1658 there
seemed a danger that the small fleet of Duke Jakob of Kurland
might fall into Russian hands, the Swedes kidnapped the duke and
occupied his territory.[1]

If the doctrine of *dominium maris* was one of the standard
arguments employed in support of Sweden's expansive foreign
policy, it was by no means the only one. There was a repertory
of them, repeated over and over again in Propositions to the Diet,
debates in the Council, and the confidential correspondence of
ministers. Their reiteration in the end induced a quasi-hypnotic
effect upon Swedish statesmen; and they formed a staple com-
ponent in domestic propaganda. They included, for instance, the
argument that on the supposition that war is in any case inevitable
it is better, safer, cheaper, less uncomfortable, to fight abroad
rather than at home: it was in virtue of this line of reasoning that
Swedish military enterprises which were considered in Stockholm
as essentially defensive in scope and intention appeared to the
outside world as examples of brutal aggression. There was the
related argument that, in the perilous situation in which Sweden
stood, it was the duty of her statesmen to avail themselves to the
uttermost of any favourable opportunity, since it might never
recur: this was an argument behind the intervention in Russia,
from 1610 to 1617; behind the attack on Denmark in 1643; behind
Oxenstierna's whole German policy after 1632; behind Charles
X's attacks on Poland in 1655 and on Denmark in 1658. It was
employed as late as 1678, on the occasion of Stenka Razin's
revolt.[2] This political pragmatism was supplemented by juridical
arguments based on *jus belli*. By right of conquest, or occupation,
or the mere deliverance of the territory of an ally from enemy
control, it was held that Sweden was entitled to retain or dispose
of the territory in question, to levy tolls and taxes, to grant fiefs
on terms of quasi-feudal subjection to the Swedish crown: in
short, a sovereign authority. It was a right firmly founded on
Grotius, which Gustav Adolf is said to have read for half an hour
every day. In practice, improbable as this may seem, it was limited
in its exercise both by prudential and by moral considerations: by
prudential, since (as we shall see below) the financing of war

---

[1] *Ibid.*, pp. 35–6.
[2] Georg Wittrock, *Karl XI:s förmyndares finanspolitik*, II (Uppsala 1917), p. 264.

depended essentially on keeping the occupied territories in a state of reasonable prosperity; by moral, since Gustav Adolf, at all events, had a conscience which was especially tender. He could on occasion authorize brutal measures of extortion and exploitation; but he agonized to a surprising extent about the legitimacy of war, made *virtus politica* his ideal,[1] and tried Oxenstierna's patience by untimely doubts whether his wars were just, and whether it could be right to make unoffending neutrals or allies suffer from the exactions of his quartermasters.[2] Lastly, there was the argument of 'reputation'. This was extraordinarily potent. One of Gustav Adolf's main charges against the Emperor was the 'scorn and ignominy' put upon Sweden by excluding its delegates from the Lübeck peace congress (where in fact they had no title to be); the Diet contributed to the war in 1627 because not to do so would involve 'the greatest disrepute' and 'an indelible shame and disgrace';[3] Oxenstierna after 1632 was never tired of reiterating, even at desperate moments, that any peace must be 'a peace with reputation'. This was not mere quixotry or chevaleresque nonsense: 'reputation', as Richelieu's *Testament* pointed out, was a fact of politics which could weigh heavily in the balance: as Erik Oxenstierna observed, it was 'the respect which preserves a country's security'.[4] Sweden herself was to experience a classic example of this truth when Brandenburg propaganda skilfully exploited the trivial military success at Fehrbellin.

The Old School, then – the school of which Nils Ahnlund was the last great representative – explained Swedish imperial expansion in terms which were essentially political. It would be erroneous and unjust to suggest that the great historians it produced were blind or indifferent to the operation of social and economic forces; but it was certainly the case that it did not occur to them that such forces had much to do with the process which they were describing. Yet even in its own terms their explanation

---

[1] For a discussion of the influence of these concepts, see Lars Gustafsson, *Virtus Politica. Politisk etik och nationellt svärmeri i den tidigare stormaktstidens litteratur* (Uppsala 1956).

[2] Styffe, *Konung Gustaf II Adolfs skrifter*, pp. 315–16.

[3] *SRARP* I.12, 31; Nils Ahnlund, *Gustaf Adolf inför tyska kriget* (Stockholm 1918), pp. 127–31, 160–1; Charles Ogier, *Från Sveriges storhetstid: Charles Ogiers dagbok under ambassaden i Sverige 1634*, ed. and trans. S. Hallberg (Stockholm 1914), pp. 98–9.

[4] *SRARP* v₂.220 (21 March 1655).

invited some criticism. It was not difficult to contend that the anticipated dangers – religious, naval, political – were exaggerated: a century ago Julius Mankell formulated this argument in terms which might have extorted a measure of agreement, if he had not spoilt his case by pushing it too far. But the Old School brushed aside his demonstration as irrelevant to the issue: what mattered, they argued, was what Swedish statesmen thought and believed and feared; and they had little difficulty in adducing massive evidence to prove that for three generations they did in fact feel the apprehensions which historians ascribed to them. Such fears may in some measure have been delusive; but that did not prevent them from being solid historical facts. There is of course no point in trying to pretend that Swedish policy down to 1660 was *exclusively* precautionary and defensive, and indeed the Old School would never have asserted as much. Obviously it was not. The argument of security exercised a compulsive fascination upon generations of Swedish statesmen; and already in 1560 the seeds had been planted of a political tradition which only a great national catastrophe would be able to uproot. Eric's objectives in going to Reval may well have been limited, and his motives precautionary; but conquests and annexations, even for defensive purposes, titillated an appetite for further acquisitions, and led him and his successors into enterprises which were effectively expansionist: as early as 1562 we find Eric engaging in intrigues designed to put him in possession of Riga. The long war with Poland began in 1600 because of the gratuitous aggression of Charles IX; the danger of Polish domination of Russia during the Time of Troubles was in large measure the result of his premature efforts to forestall it; the War of Kalmar was mainly due to his rash provocations. The attacks on Denmark in 1643 and 1658 were acts of aggression likewise. Yet, as seen from Stockholm, all these wars were defensive: they were forced upon Sweden by considerations strategic or financial. No doubt contemporaries would have smiled sardonically at the suggestion that Sweden made war in self-defence. They saw Sweden as a repeated aggressor; they resented the imperious tone and arrogant manners which Swedish statesmen, flushed with victory, increasingly adopted. 'The Gascons of the North', a French ambassador called them; and Louis XIV would find their pretensions to equality hard to stomach.[1] D'Avaux reported of Johan Oxenstierna at the Congress of Westphalia that he behaved as though he was sitting enthroned to judge the twelve tribes of Israel.[2] But Axel Oxenstierna, after all, had seriously contemplated getting himself made Elector of Mainz. And Per Brahe, whose great county of Visingsö was bigger (and better run) than many a petty German state,[3] considered himself as fully the equal of a German prince. Johan Oxenstierna did no more than take his tone from his father – and, indeed, from his sovereign: by 1650 Christina was insisting on the new title of 'Majesty',[4] with a tart reminder to her Council that 'Things have much altered in the world since King Gustav and King Eric were in it.'[5] A Queen of Sweden was now set high above the world's judgment; as Monaldesco would discover. She spent much of the rest of her life underlining the point, to the irritation of the Roman aristocracy and the embarrassment of the Curia.

These examples are in fact no more than indications of a deep national psychological need: the need for self-assertion in the face of a world unaccustomed to think that the Swedes were of much account in it. It is seen in their prickly pride in their language, which appears in such diverse characters as Olof Petri, John III (who once rebuked the impertinence of a king who wrote to him in French by answering him in Finnish), 'Skogekär Bergbo' (who pleaded for a Swedish purged of foreign accretions) and Axel Oxenstierna, who waged war on the unnecessary use of German in official documents.[6] It lay behind Eric XIV's creation of counts and barons, that Swedish diplomats might not be at a social

[1] C.-G. Picavet, *La Diplomatie française au temps de Louis XIV* (Paris 1930), pp. 151, 190.

[2] C. T. Odhner, *Sveriges inre historia under Drottning Christinas förmyndare* (Stockholm 1865), p. 199.

[3] For the semi-regal rule of Per Brahe on Visingsö, see Robert Swedlund, *Grev- och friherreskapen i Sverige och Finland. Donationerna och reduktionerna före 1680* (Uppsala 1936), pp. 187–8, 198.

[4] It was not as new as she thought: Eric XIV had exacted it too.

[5] *RRP* XIV.321 (1 October 1650).

[6] For a typical example, see K. R. Melander, *Die Beziehungen Lübecks zu Schweden und Verhandlungen dieser beiden Staaten wegen des russischen Handels über Reval und Narva während der Jahre 1643–53* (Helsingfors 1903), p. 27.

disadvantage when dealing with foreign dignitaries. It appears in
the refusal of Swedish Lutheranism in the seventeenth century to
be guided by German theologians, or to involve itself in their
unedifying controversies: it was rather for Helmstedt or Witten-
berg to give a respectful attention to the divines of the greatest
Lutheran state in Europe. It explains the demand, in 1668, for the
introduction of a distinctive national costume (at least for the
nobility): other nations, said the *lantmarskalk*, had their own
national dress, and shall we 'who are so glorious and renowned
a nation...let ourselves be led by the nose by a parcel of French
dancing-masters?'[1] An intense national pride, joined to an uncomfortable sense of national inferiority, explain much that is
repellent in the men of the seventeenth century: without some
sympathetic understanding of it, no true appreciation of the Age
of Greatness is possible.

If to other nations the Swedes appeared as bellicose and
bullying, they could scarcely complain. For they certainly showed
a strong tendency to take belligerence as their own peculiar way
of life. It was the youthful Charles X, pleading to be allowed to
see army service, who wrote 'Sweden's greatness rests above all
on war';[2] but the remark might equally well have been made by
any Swedish statesman after 1632, and was indeed made by more
than one of them. And it was Queen Christina, who in 1648 had
posed before the world as the humane bringer of peace to
distracted Europe, who in 1652 told the Nobility:

A war is better than a disgraceful peace. For who would live in
thraldom? Our rise has come through war. It were an eternal disgrace
to our position and our country if others saw that we took no better
care of our interests; and we should be inexcusable to our
posterity...When therefore we see the danger, and know too that God
has commanded His people to wage war, why shall we not do it?[3]

If peace came, how could the state cope with disbanded noble
officers, thrown suddenly upon the world without employment?
In 1660 there were said to be no less than 800 such persons. No
wonder that the swashbuckling Schlippenbach shook his head,

[1] *SRARP* x.100 (22 June 1668).
[2] H. Rosengren, *Karl Gustaf före tronbestigningen* (Stockholm 1913), p. 135.
[3] *SRARP* v$_1$.116 (2 November 1652); and *cf.* a similar remark to the Council in
1650: *RRP* XIV.307.

and feared that 'eine gefährliche Verstopfung *in regni Intestinis* darauf erfolgen möchte'.[1]

This suggests another explanation of Swedish imperialism, which we may pause to consider before proceeding to the more substantial theories of the New School. Is it possible that the argument from security was no more than a convenient cloak for the interests of a small exploitative class? that the empire was acquired because it suited the aristocracy to acquire it? that, in short, the explanation of Swedish expansion is not so much political as social; and that religious bigotry, Gothicist propaganda and bogus arguments shed a false lustre over the whole nefarious business? This was the view of Axel Strindberg, who in his tendentious style wrote that the wars were 'a feudal-inspired action to secure and extend their [the nobility's] landed property, and shut the mouth of complaining peasants, and other trouble-some commoners'.[2] It is true that not many historians have been inclined to follow him: but there are sufficient grains of truth in the theory to give it a modicum of plausibility: as Professor Åström wrote, 'a war economy worked to the advantage of the ruling classes, and not only the generals, but also those – the regents, the high aristocracy – who above all found their advan-tage in an active foreign policy'.[3] The continual wars did indeed offer the impoverished nobleman (and most noblemen were in comparatively modest circumstances) the prospect of a career – a better career than his lack of learning could open for him in the civil service, and an agreeable alternative to hunting and coursing for many *knapar* who otherwise would 'sit at home and drink tobacco'. But we should not forget that the wars also entailed the expensive obligation of knight-service, the erosion of the nobility's fiscal immunities, the loss of their labour-force to the conscription. Not many of them, one suspects, came home from

---

[1] F. F. Carlson, *Sveriges historia under konungarne af det pfalziska huset* (Stockholm 1883), II, p. 79 *n* 1.

[2] Axel Strindberg, *Bondenöd och stormaktsdröm* (Stockholm 1937), p. 135. *Cf.* Jan Peters, 'Unter der schwedischen Krone', *Zeitschrift für Geschichtswissenschaft*, XIV (1966), p. 41: 'Der Wunsch, Einfluss auf die deutschen Reichsangelegenheiten zu nehmen, entsprach den in der Grossmachtspolitik zum Ausdruck kommenden feudal-expansiven Zielen der herrschenden Klasse in Schweden.'

[3] S.-E. Åström, 'The Swedish Economy', in *Sweden's Age of Greatness*, ed. M. Roberts (1973), p. 73.

the wars much richer than when they set out: not for them the fat church lands of Bremen, the lucrative jobs on the provincial military or civil establishment, the vast *latifundia* in the Baltic provinces, which rewarded the great nobles and the senior commanders. Only twice, as far as I am aware, did a monarch expressly dangle before the nobility the prospect of rich rewards overseas. The first time was in 1617, *after* the peace of Stolbova, when Gustav Adolf tried to interest them in colonizing the provinces which Sweden had just taken from the Russians.[1] The second was in 1654, when Charles X promised those Pomeranian nobles whose estates had been reduced in order to form Queen Christina's dower lands that they should receive compensation – in Poland.[2] Otherwise, he and his successors were in the habit of appealing (not in vain) not to the nobility's greed and ambition, but to its sense of duty and its patriotism.

It is obvious, nevertheless, that there must have been many nobles, condemned by peace to obscurity, who heartily wished that the war would begin again. But there were others who had been anxious enough to end it while it was raging. It is worth recalling that throughout almost the whole period of the creation of the empire there was domestic opposition to the policy of expansion. It came, of course, from those who had to pay the taxes. But it found supporters too among the nobility: often very eminent supporters indeed. When in John III's reign Sweden for the first time began to get a secure grip on Estonia, the nobility showed little interest in the prospect of acquiring colonial estates once the conquest was secure: on the contrary, they vainly pressed the king to put an end to the whole enterprise, on the ground that Sweden was too exhausted to carry it on.[3] Neither the nobility nor any other Estate welcomed Charles IX's provocative invasion of Livonia; and when he seemed set on a collision course

---

[1] *Tal och skrifter av Konung Gustav II Adolf*, ed. Carl Hallendorff (Stockholm 1915), pp. 46–53: English translation in M. Roberts, *Sweden as a Great Power. Government: Society: Foreign Policy* (London 1968), pp. 134–5.

[2] G. H. von Essen, *Alienationer och reduktioner i f.d. svenska Pommern* (Stockholm 1900), p. 47.

[3] Sven A. Nilsson, *Kampen om de adliga privilegierna 1526–1594* (Lund 1952), p. 66; *Svenska riksdagsakter* (*SRDA*) i.ii.577–8; iii.825; Åke Hermansson, *Karl IX och ständerna* (Uppsala 1962), pp. 116–18. Though that slippery customer Hogenskild Bielke was anxious to get his share of donations in Estonia: Sven A. Nilsson, *Krona och frälse i Sverige, 1523–1594* (Lund 1947), p. 367.

with Denmark in 1610, it was the nobles of the Council who roundly told him that another war was 'intolerable and impossible'.[1] Karl Karlsson Gyllenhielm was all for getting out of the Russian war in 1616; Johan Skytte would have got out of the Polish war in 1622.[2] For the best part of two decades Gabriel Gustafsson Oxenstierna sprinkled his letters to his brother the chancellor with sighs for peace and gloomy descriptions of the country's sufferings: 'the common man wishes himself dead'; 'we may indeed say that we have conquered lands from others, and to that end ruined our own'; 'the branches expand; the tree withers at the roots'.[3] Karl Karlsson Gyllenhielm, Jakob de la Gardie, Johan Skytte, Johan Adler Salvius formed in the mid-thirties a loosely-associated group which was bound together by (among other things) a wish for peace, a readiness to sacrifice gains in Prussia to obtain it, and an almost frantic desire to get out of the German imbroglio on nearly any terms. Klas Fleming held similar views.[4] Only the return of Axel Oxenstierna in 1636 availed to brace the nerve of the Regents and stiffen the resolve of the Council to go on fighting. It is significant that the elements opposed to Axel Oxenstierna thought it good tactics to try to brand him as a war-monger.[5] Yet in the years after Nördlingen Oxenstierna would have been glad of peace in Germany if he could have had it on acceptable terms; and when he renewed the French alliance in 1638 that was not the alternative he would have preferred. He did not continue the struggle in Germany, any more than Gustav Adolf began it, because it was to the benefit of a privileged class. No doubt within limits it was so; it provided opportunities to acquire crown lands and revenues on what were

---

[1] E. W. Bergman, *Register öfver Rådslag i Konung Karl IX:s tid* (Stockholm 1883), *sub* December 1610 and *cf. ibid.*, *sub* 18 May 1610; W. Tham, *Axel Oxenstierna. Hans ungdom och verksamhet intill år 1612* (Stockholm 1935), pp. 229–30.

[2] *AOSB* II.x.17, 260.

[3] *AOSB* II.iii.42, 44–5, 169–71, 193, 196; *Handlingar rörande Skandinaviens historia* XXXII (1851), pp. 273–4; Sune Lundgren, *Johan Adler Salvius* (Lund 1945), p. 111.

[4] *RRP* II.144–7; Georg Wittrock, *Regering och allmoge under Drottning Kristinas förmyndare* (Uppsala 1948), p. 80; *SRARP* II.193, 218–19.

[5] The accusation was apparently a serviceable political weapon as late as 1651, when the younger Messenius used it: *RRP* xv.223. On 15 June 1656 D'Avaugour wrote to Mazarin: 'On m'assure que la plus grande part de ses [*sc.* Charles X's] Sénateurs n'ambitionne pas seulement de le voir en paix, mais aussi le voir désarmé et retourné en son royaume.' Carlson, *Sveriges historia*, I, pp. 195–6 *n* 1.

really, if not formally, attractive terms. But the Regency alienated them only after long hesitation, and with many qualms about their constitutional right to do so during a minority; and we must not confuse cause and effect. It may well be true that some of those who championed the cause of peace did so for reasons which were related to domestic struggles for power rather than to genuinely differing views of foreign policy. But there was none the less among the nobility a long tradition of opposition to imperial expansion. It went back to the meeting at Reval in 1589, and was to continue with the opposition of Herman Fleming and Carl Mörner to the wars of Charles X.[1] That tradition was never more plainly expressed than in Gustaf Bonde's *Memorial* of 1661; which said flatly that the overseas provinces had been too dearly bought in terms of men and money, and added 'The more we acquire, the poorer we become, since none of the provinces can support itself.'[2] And the end-term of this tradition comes with Anders Nordencrantz, who in the 1760s denounced the whole imperial experience as a disastrous mistake.[3]

It will not do, then, to think simply in terms of a nobility eager for the spoils of empire. There was among them a strong anti-imperial tradition. True, it availed very little, even at Reval in 1589. But the explanation of why that should have been so provides the best reply to the theory of a class-motivated imperialism. It is, quite simply, that in the great decisions which pushed Sweden along the imperial path the Estate of Nobility had very little share. For the decisions were mostly the king's, and his alone. To this point I shall return in the next chapter.

I turn now to a consideration of the view of the New School of historians upon these problems. That school has produced an alternative explanation of the creation of the empire: an explanation which would dismiss political considerations as almost irrelevant, or at least would relegate them to a subordinate place. It is a view which owes its origin to that great scholar Ingvar

---

[1] See *SRARP* v₂.207–27.

[2] Georg Wittrock, 'Gustaf Bondes politiska program', *Historisk tidskrift (HT)* 1913, pp. 45–6: English translation of this passage in Roberts, *Sweden as a Great Power*, pp. 173–4.

[3] [Anders Nordencrantz] *Tankar om Krig i gemen och Sveriges Krig i synnerhet* (Stockholm 1767), I, pp. 43–4.

Andersson, who first launched it in his studies of the life and reign of Eric XIV; it has been developed and systematized by Artur Attman; and it has now become an orthodoxy.[1] It asserts that the motive behind Swedish expansion was not political but economic; that Swedish policy, from Eric XIV onwards (if not, indeed, from Gustav Vasa) was consciously directed to the securing of a monopoly of the trade between Muscovy and the West. Russian timber and hemp built the fleet which defeated the Armada; Polish and Lithuanian grain, with its great staple market at Amsterdam, supplied the growing deficiencies of western Europe and the Mediterranean lands. Swedish expansion was designed to control this trade and levy dues upon it; to supplant the decaying Hanse in their historic *rôle* of middlemen and purveyors. Thus the Swedish Empire was, after all, an empire of exploitation and enterprise, though not of private enterprise. Its natural goals were Narva, Reval, Riga and eventually also Königsberg and Danzig; the end-ports of the Eastland trade. The theory was put in its extremest form by Sven Svensson, in his study of the mercantile background to the Russian attack upon Livonia, when he wrote: 'The attempt to control the Russian market was from beginning to end the alpha and omega of Swedish Baltic policy.'[2]

It is not difficult to find plenty of evidence which appears to support this thesis. Gustav Vasa, Eric XIV, John III, all undoubtedly would have liked to channel the trade to Russia through Swedish-controlled ports; and all three made the attempt. Christian II had had similar ideas in 1520. The experiences of 1558–9, when for a brief period the staple of the trade had been fixed at Viborg, offered impressive testimony to the increase in customs-revenues which could result from such an arrangement: in 1551 the value of imports from Russia to Viborg was 74,000 marks; in 1559 it rose to more than 506,000 marks; in 1563, when Viborg had been replaced as the staple by Narva, it had fallen to

[1] Ingvar Andersson, *Erik XIV:s engelska underhandlingar* (Lund 1935); Artur Attman, *Den ryska marknaden i 1500-talets baltiska politik* (Lund 1944); and Per Nyström's important article 'Mercatura Ruthenica', *Scandia* 1937. Not least, it would seem, among Soviet historians: see Ingmar Oldberg's review of *Istorija Švecii*, ed. A. S. Kan (Moscow 1974), in *HT* 1976, p. 79.
[2] Sven Svensson, *Den merkantila bakgrunden till Rysslands anfall på livländska ordensstaten* (Lund 1951), p. 10.

less than 13,000.[1] The Russian capture of Narva precipitated a rush of traders to that port, where for the first time they had direct access to the Russian market without being mulcted by Hanseatic middlemen. Narva did indeed pass into Swedish hands in 1581; but its place was to some extent supplied by the opening of the White Sea route in 1553, and the foundation of Archangel thirty years later. It therefore became an aim of Swedish policy, first clearly formulated by John III, and never forgotten thereafter, to force the trade back to Estonian or Ingrian ports by blocking the White Sea route and capturing Archangel. John III, Charles IX, Gustav Adolf, Charles XII, all made abortive expeditions against Archangel. Geographically and politically Sweden might erect a barrier to Russian expansion; but it proved no barrier to trade, which simply by-passed it – to the south, as well as to the north. Hence (it is argued) just as Sweden tried to block the northern alternative by seizing Archangel, so too she tried to control the routes to south and west. It is this which explains the taking of Riga in 1621, the occupation of the Vistula delta and the threat to Königsberg and Danzig after 1626, the invasion of Kurland in 1658, and the ultimata to Duke Jakob a decade later,[2] when Sweden forced Duke Jakob to abandon a project for a canal from the Düna to Libau, by-passing Riga.

It is certainly true that successive Swedish rulers indulged in grandiose commercial project-making, and dreamed of great trade-routes which should link Swedish-controlled Baltic ports, through the Russian river-system, to Persia and Central Asia. From Charles IX's time onwards, Persian ambassadors turned up at irregular intervals in Stockholm; des Hayes de Cormenin was sent by Richelieu to propose a great consortium which should channel the Persia trade through Narva;[3] Axel Oxenstierna was interested in a similar scheme emanating from the Duke of Holstein–Gottorp;[4] Charles XI brought Armenian merchants to

[1] Artur Attman, *The Russian and Polish Markets in International Trade 1560–1650* (Göteborg 1973), p. 67. For Gustav Vasa's interest, see *Gustav Vasas Registratur*, XXI.44, 57.

[2] Georg Wittrock, *Karl XI:s förmyndares finanspolitik*, II, p. 90.

[3] For Des Hayes de Cormenin, see A. Tongas, *L'Ambassadeur Louis Deshayes de Cormenin* (Paris 1937); cf. David Norrman, *Gustav Adolfs politik mot Ryssland och Polen under tyska kriget* (Uppsala 1943), pp. 14–15.

[4] *AOSB* I.ix.175: xi.187.

Stockholm, to discuss the possibilities in that part of the world.[1] To the end of the period economic objectives of this sort remained prominent features of Swedish policy. Nevertheless, it must at once be said that generalizations such as Svensson's, purporting to apply to the whole period of Swedish imperialism, cannot be accepted. There were, no doubt, moments when the economic motive was so important as to be predominant; but there were many others when it was clearly subordinate. Eric XIV's project (if it was really his) for a Russia trade based on English capital and a Swedish staple, and avoiding the Sound Dues by a canal through central Sweden – this was at best a loose idea, loosely thrown out to tickle Elizabeth's ear.[2] No effort was made to translate it into terms of practical politics; and Eric's foreign policy would probably have been unaffected if it had never been formulated. The more balanced treatment of Eric's reign which Ingvar Andersson's classic biography inaugurated has perhaps led historians to take too seriously what was no more than the oratorical flourish of an ambassador; and I suggest, with great respect, that the available evidence will not bear the weight which Ingvar Andersson laid upon it: it is worth recalling that Kjell Kumlien and Gunnar Annell long ago, from their very different standpoints, expressed reservations in this regard.[3]

Under John III the situation was rather different. Eric had been Russia's friend (the first to choose that option); John fought the Russians for a quarter of a century. His armies took Narva; and in the 1580s Sweden for the first time obtained a really firm grip upon Estonia. Meanwhile the White Sea route was developed by Dutch and English, and John reacted to the challenge by attempting to capture Archangel. It is clear that for him his actions in the Arctic and the Baltic formed complementary halves of the same foreign policy; and to control the Russia trade was certainly one element in that policy. Yet it was not the only element, nor even, perhaps, the main one. In regard to the Arctic, for instance,

[1] Harald Hjärne, *Karl XII. Omstörtningen i Östersjön 1697–1703* (Stockholm 1902), p. 28.
[2] For a discussion of this point, see M. Roberts, *The Early Vasas* (Cambridge 1968), pp. 160–2, where the crucial source is printed, from *Gustav Vasas Registratur*, XXIX.850.
[3] Knell Kumlien, *Sverige och Hanseaterna* (Stockholm 1953), pp. 257, 260, 449; Gunnar Annell, *Erik XIV:s etiska föreställningar och deras inflytande på hans politik* (Uppsala 1945).

one element in it was to deprive the Russians of the right to tax the wandering Lapps. Hitherto, Denmark, Sweden and Muscovy had each taken a third share of the Lapp-tax: in 1588 John, in virtue of his victories in Livonia, claimed and appropriated the Russian third; and the peace of Teusina, which for the first time provided for a clearly defined frontier to the east extending to the Arctic sea, did not disturb that claim. In regard to Livonia, the need to secure supplies for the Swedish armies fighting in Estonia led John to attempt to interfere with the free export of grain from Narva and Reval; and that attempt, if it had not been resisted, would have driven the trade to the Livonian ports of Riga and Pernau. The debasement of the Swedish currency which occurred in the 1570s and 1580s tended to the same consequence. As long as these alternative routes through Livonia lay outside the areas of Swedish domination there was always the danger that military needs, or domestic policies, would drive the trade away from Swedish control. From a purely economic point of view, therefore, the acquisition of Livonia became an intelligible Swedish objective.[1] In the course of negotiations for a truce in 1583 John put forward demands which certainly appear to have far-reaching economic implications – demands far in excess of anything warranted by the actual military situation. His negotiators asked for the cession of Novgorod, Pskov, Gdov, Ladoga, Porchov and Nöteborg – that is, of the great distributing centres from which the ports of Estonia and Livonia were supplied. It may be that these terms represent 'a new aspiration for the future, a sudden enlargement of Swedish ambitions, a programme of conquest which would not be forgotten'.[2] But it is difficult to believe that they were more than an extreme bargaining-position, put forward to meet the equally unrealistic claims which (as past and future experience made clear) could be expected to be advanced from the Russian side; and on the whole it may be doubted whether economic considerations were the essential determinant of John's

[1] Artur Attman, 'Till det svenska östersjöväldets problematik', in *Studier tillägnade Curt Weibull* (Göteborg 1946), *passim*, and p. 78, where he writes that the frontier between Swedish Estonia and Polish Livonia 'cut across the economic triangle Narva–Reval–Riga', and until this situation was rectified 'it was impossible for Swedish statesmen to realize the economic ideas which were the driving-force behind Sweden's Baltic policy'.

[2] Roberts, *The Early Vasas*, p. 265.

policy. What he really wanted was to expel the Russians from Estonia, and to finance the operation from the customs-dues on the Russia trade. In order to push the Russians back from the sea he was prepared for friendship, military collaboration, and at last dynastic union with Poland; though from a purely commercial point of view Poland was Sweden's rival. The Swedish–Polish commonwealth of which John believed he had laid the foundations was a *political* design, directed against Russia. True, it might be expected if fully implemented to solve the problem of alternative trade-routes through the Livonian ports; but it would also solve the much more immediate problem of the security of Sweden's eastern frontier. Alliance with Poland against Russia was, after all, a political option which John III was not alone in making: it would have been the preferred choice of Charles X in 1655; it was the basis of the policy of Charles XII after 1702; and on neither of these two later occasions was the decision based on economic motives. Not without reason did Professor Attman once remark to me that it is reasonable to place the beginnings of Sweden's Age of Greatness in the aspirations of John III.[1]

But already before John's reign had reached its melancholy conclusion it was apparent that neither his political nor his economic designs were likely to be realized. The idea of a Swedish–Polish commonwealth broke down almost from the beginning – not least because Poland coveted Reval quite as much as Sweden desired Riga. The expedition against Archangel proved a fiasco. At the peace of Teusina in 1595 the Tsar did indeed admit Sweden's right to Estonia, and he did recognize Reval and Viborg as staples for the Russia trade;[2] but the effect of this last concession was only that the trade at its southern end leaked away, as before, through Pskov and Riga, and at its northern end continued to flow through Archangel.[3]

---

[1] In conversation, June 1976.

[2] Helge Almquist, *Sverige och Ryssland 1595–1613* (Uppsala 1907), p. 15.

[3] Attman, *Russian and Polish Markets*, ch. II. It seems possible that Swedish policy may have been based on a misconception of the real nature of the Russia trade – that is, on the belief that the Baltic ports and Archangel were in some sense real alternatives; whereas each may have served a different trade and a different market, and exports could not readily be switched from one to the other. This view has however been vigorously contested by Attman, it being central to his thesis that the Russia trade was a unity. His argument is persuasive; but this is a controversy upon which it would be imprudent for a layman to intrude.

What was true of John III was also in great measure true of
Charles IX. Once again Baltic and Arctic politics are linked; an
aggressive thrust towards a warm-water port near the modern
Narvik goes hand in hand with a blockade of Riga and military
intervention in Russia – this time not as Poland's ally, but as her
enemy. But it is to be observed that Riga was blockaded not so
much to force trade to Reval and Narva, but rather as a means
of inflicting injury on Poland; that the intervention in Russia had
clearly political and dynastic aims; and that the Arctic policy was
primarily concerned, not with the Russia trade, but with finding
a way round the barrier of the Sound.

Now it is true that in 1613 Gustav Adolf put forward
peace-terms to the Russians which have been adduced to lend
support to the 'economic' thesis, and which are strikingly similar
to those propounded by John III in 1583. He asked also that no
foreign nation, other than Sweden, be allowed to conduct trade
in Russia through the Baltic, and that only Swedes have the right
to export Russian goods through Baltic ports.[1] But these demands,
extravagant as they may seem, were not pressed; and the peace
of Stolbova did not incorporate them. This led Professor Attman
to the paradoxical conclusion that that peace was in fact a
disappointment, almost a reverse, because it did nothing to further
the economic domination of the trade with the West.[2] In fact,
it did not fit the Attman model, and *therefore* was a setback. But
it could equally well be argued that it is evidence that the Attman
thesis is not of general validity. The most recent study of Swedish
opinion in the period before the peace suggests that though there
are indeed plenty of references to commercial considerations, they
are clearly much subordinate to political and strategic objectives.[3]
Gustav Adolf, one suspects, would have given short shrift to
Attman's interpretation: his speech to the Estates at the coronation
riksdag of 1617 is a paean of victory; it is eloquent on Sweden's
strategic and political gains; but it gives only a minor place to the
Russia trade.[4] It is true that when the Swedish delegation went
to Moscow to ratify the peace it bore with it instructions to try

[1] Hallenberg, *Svea Rikes Historia*, II, pp. 33–5; Attman, 'Freden i Stolbova 1617.
En aspekt', *Scandia* 1949.
[2] Attman, 'Freden i Stolbova', *passim*.
[3] Tarkiainen, 'Faran från öst' p. 36.
[4] English translation in Roberts, *Sweden as a Great Power*, pp. 134–6.

to arrange a package-deal which should include both an anti-Polish alliance and a commercial agreement (which would, however, have fallen far short of the monopoly which Gustav Adolf had demanded in 1613);[1] but nevertheless one gets the strong impression that he saw the settlement of 1617 primarily in political and strategic rather than in economic terms.

The peace of Stolbova marks the moment when Swedish expansion began to gather momentum. It was followed in the third decade of the century by the taking of Riga, the conquest of Livonia, the transference of the seat of war to Prussia, and the beginning of the long involvement in Germany. How far are these developments explicable in economic terms? The answer, it seems, must be 'only to a very limited extent'. Gustav Adolf certainly said on one occasion that 'Sweden's welfare depends, under God, upon trade and maritime commerce'; and Axel Oxenstierna was undoubtedly anxious to attract the Russia trade to Swedish-controlled ports in the Baltic provinces.[2] But as regards the Polish war the object was to force Sigismund III to recognize the legitimacy of Gustav Adolf's tenure of the Swedish throne, to compel him to renounce his own claims, and to make peace; and the Livonian and Prussian campaigns are to be seen as attempts to do this by tying up the main arteries of Lithuanian and Polish exports – the Düna and the Vistula. Both sides, in fact, were employing the tactics of economic warfare; and Sigismund's reply to the capture of Riga was to try to cut it off from its hinterland. Much fresh light on Gustav Adolf's Polish policy has been shed by the publication in 1974 of Axel Norberg's excellent dissertation on Swedish–Polish relations between 1617 and 1626, a dissertation which has a good claim to be considered the most significant contribution to the debate on the king's foreign policy to appear for forty years. And it is curious to observe with what anxious care the author seeks to safeguard himself against any suspicion that he may not whole-heartedly subscribe to the now-dominant orthodoxy. A section of his introduction dutifully rehearses it; again and again our attention is called to the fact that commercial motives 'may well'[3] have

[1] Axel Norberg, *Polen i svensk politik 1617–1626* (Stockholm 1974), pp. 50–1.

[2] E.g. *AOSB* I.v.203; xi.189.

[3] A beautifully cautious formulation appears on p. 131 of Norberg's *Polen i svensk politik:* 'Bakom de expansionistiska motiven *torde bl. a* ha legat en förhoppning om att vinna kontroll över transithandeln genom Livland [my italics].'

had an influence on policy. But once this obligatory homage has been paid, once the decent obeisances have been made, Norberg (despite discreetly-phrased reservations which tend to amount to very little) proceeds without flinching to the conclusions which his evidence imposes on him; and they are not, alas, conclusions which support the economic thesis. As he himself frankly acknowledges, there is simply not enough evidence about the trade of Livonia to shed any helpful light on Gustav Adolf's intentions: a pity, he remarks, but there it is.[1] And he takes great care to emphasize that old-fashioned considerations such as strategy and security were of great – perhaps of prime – importance: 'One must not' (he observes, with refreshing candour) – 'one must not exaggerate the significance of possible commercial motives simply because Gustav Adolf was not merely seeking a peace or truce, but was also looking for conquests. For conquests were seen as being of significance to a policy of security.'[2] To which eminently sensible observation one can only add the comment 'O si sic omnes!'

It really will not do, then, to write (as Sven Lundkvist does) that after the acquisition of Kexholm and Ingria Sweden's 'next objective must logically be Riga', and that its capture 'represented one more step on the road towards control of the Russia trade'.[3] It was indeed logical, on the somewhat rash assumption that Gustav Adolf's mind worked like the minds of those who seek now to interpret it; but it was no less logical if all he wanted was to force Sigismund to make peace. At the meeting of the Council in March 1621 which endorsed the king's decision to attack Poland, considerations of economic expansionism do not seem to have been ventilated at all.[4] And one wonders what the modern school makes of Gustav Adolf's promise to Riga at the time of its capitulation to ensure that its privileges should remain intact, in the event of its being handed back to Poland. For indeed, in the first years after 1621, as Ragnar Liljedahl long ago observed, retrocession was 'by no means a far-fetched idea'.[5] Norberg

---

[1] Ibid., p. 26.
[2] Ibid., p. 113.
[3] Sven Lundkvist, 'The Experience of Empire', p. 30.
[4] Norberg, Polen i svensk politik, pp. 112–13.
[5] Ragnar Liljedahl, Svensk förvaltning i Livland 1617–1634 (Uppsala 1933), pp. 72, 170. And Hallenberg before him: Jonas Hallenberg, Svea Rikes Historia, v, pp. 42–4.

makes this point with greater emphasis than ever before.[1] In 1622 Gustav Adolf was willing to restore Riga in return for a peace which incorporated Sigismund's renunciation of his claims to the Swedish throne. He was willing to restore it in return for a truce of fifty years, provided that the Poles either paid a war-indemnity, or left him in possession of five other towns of essentially *strategic* importance. He was even willing to restore it as one of the terms of a peace between himself and the Polish Republic from which Sigismund should be altogether excluded. A year later, in 1623, he was still prepared for the retrocession of Riga if he could get a settlement which gave him security. Thus for purely political reasons he would have handed back what was to become the greatest city in the Swedish empire (and both he and Oxenstierna held that flourishing towns were essential to the welfare of the state, and the more the better); and he would have renounced all the obvious fiscal and commercial advantages which its possession would bring him. In the face of these facts, how is it possible to maintain that the driving-force behind Swedish foreign policy was a consistent determination to control the Russia trade? Certainly no such determination lay behind the transference of the seat of war to Prussia in 1626, though on the economic-expansionist theory no doubt it ought to have done. It is certainly true that the large financial benefits which accrued from the taking of toll at the ports of Livonia and Prussia had by 1629 become a matter of high importance: the mounting cost of war, and the imminence of a greater struggle which might be expected to be costlier still, necessarily made it so.[2] But they valued these 'licences' mainly because they furnished the means for pursuing by arms ends which were political rather than economic: it is worth remarking that the whole yield of the licences was devoted to the payment of the armies in Germany. And if Gustav Adolf was anxious in 1628 to '*conjungere littora maris Balthici*', his object was not to control the Russia trade, but to 'keep an open door, both in winter and summer, for free access and withdrawal' of troops.[3]

---

[1] Norberg, *Polen i svensk politik*, pp. 159–62.

[2] This is evident perhaps for the first time in *RRP* I.128 (23 April 1629): contrast, e.g., Gabriel Gustafsson Oxenstierna in *SRARP* I.14 (23 January 1627).

[3] *AOSB* II.i.398 (to Axel Oxenstierna, 1 April 1628).

The intervention in Germany provides an interesting example of how far the economic-expansionist explanation has been accepted, and how untenable it can be. That admirable economic historian, Kurt Samuelsson, in his lively sketch of Sweden's social development, *From Great Power to Welfare State*, confronts the startled reader with the following passage:

> Ostensibly Gustavus II Adolphus and Axel Oxenstierna entered the war on religious grounds; but *as the willing support of Cardinal Richelieu's Catholic France demonstrated* the conflict developed into a struggle for markets and financial positions [my italics].[1]

Even those who are disposed to see in Richelieu a budding Colbert blighted by an unkind fate would hardly swallow this staggering *non-sequitur*. I cannot guess at what date the conflict may be supposed to have 'developed into a struggle for markets and financial positions': if before 1636, it has left singularly little trace in Oxenstierna's correspondence; if afterwards, it would be interesting to know what markets Banér had in mind when he fought the battle of Wittstock, or Torstensson when he fought the battle of Janków; and also the precise bearing of these economic plans upon the uneasy relationship of Sweden and her French ally. All the evidence suggests that Gustav Adolf did not invade Germany to obtain control of the Baltic ports; he used control of the Baltic ports to finance his invasion: such, at all events, was the verdict of Axel Oxenstierna in 1650;[2] and I am disposed to believe him. The ports of Pomerania and Mecklenburg had certainly no relevance to the control of the Russia trade; but they had great relevance as invasion-bases. And indeed it is a hard matter to try to show that the primary aim of Swedish foreign policy in the years after 1630 was the economic domination of the Baltic: almost as perverse as to suggest that Gustav Adolf conquered Germany in order to find a vent for Swedish copper.[3] Relations with Russia in the early thirties did indeed bring the

[1] Kurt Samuelsson, *From Great Power to Welfare State* (London 1968), p. 15. The original Swedish avoids the *non-sequitur* (which presumably, however, must have received the author's sanction in the translation), and says merely that the war 'blev på liknande sätt i hög grad ett krig för ekonomiska och finansiella positioner'.

[2] *RRP* XIV.472 (1650).

[3] As Friedrich Bothe did: *Gustaf Adolf und seine Kanzlers wirtschaftspolitische Absichten auf Deutschland* (Frankfurt 1910).

Tsar's concession of a monopoly of the sale of Russian grain in Amsterdam – an episode which led Porshnev to far-reaching (but quite unwarranted) conclusions about Russia's contribution to Gustav Adolf's victories;[1] but this was a very temporary affair, made possible by exceptionally high prices in Amsterdam owing to a shortage of Polish grain,[2] and in any case it was part of the agreement that the grain be shipped from *Archangel*. When in October 1633 Oxenstierna sent home his views on a Russian proposal for an alliance, he mentioned every conceivable consideration save one: there was not a word about the Russia trade.[3] When in 1634 the Estates were invited to consider the proposal, the chance of trading advantages came seventh and last among the arguments advanced in support of the idea.[4] When Axel Oxenstierna in January 1635 listed the reasons against retroceding West Prussia to Poland in return for a long truce, or a peace, the revenues from tolls at Prussian ports likewise took fourth place to strategic and political considerations.[5] It is no doubt true that when by the truce of Stuhmsdorf in that year Prussia was in fact retroceded Oxenstierna in his anger declared that Sweden was not half the nation she had been before the truce was concluded;[6] but by this he meant that the capacity to fight in Germany (and to defend herself from Poland) had been gravely impaired – not that the master-plan of Swedish statesmanship had been departed from. His whole attitude to the Prussian question, and to the possibility of relinquishing Sweden's claim to Pomerania in exchange for compensation in Prussia, was in fact heavily loaded by purely political considerations: anxiety to avoid offending Brandenburg; fear of leaving invasion-ports in the Vistula delta in Polish hands, at a time when the succession in Sweden hung upon the life of a far-from-robust child.[7]

[1] B. Porshnev, 'Les rapports politiques de l'Europe occidentale et de l'Europe orientale à l'époque de la guerre de trente ans' (xie Congrès International des Sciences Historiques, Stockholm 1960, Rapports IV, pp. 136–63). The original agreement is printed in *RRP* I.164. Porshnev's theories have been convincingly refuted in Lars Ekholm, 'Rysk spannmål och svenska krigsfinanser 1629–1633', *Scandia* 1974.

[2] Attman, *Russian and Polish Markets*, p. 89 *n* 183.

[3] *AOSB* I.x.28.   [4] *SRARP* II.51.

[5] *AOSB* I.xiii.32.   [6] *AOSB* I.xiv.136.

[7] *AOSB* I.xiii, *passim*; *Handlingar rörande Skandinaviens Historia* XXXII (1851), p. 281; Herbert Rettig, *Die Stellung des Regierung und des Reichstages Schwedens zum polnischen Frage* (Halle 1916).

Arnold Soom, it seems to me, was clearly right in regarding Oxenstierna's economic strategy after 1626 as a response to the needs of war, rather than the motive that inspired it.[1] After his return home in 1636 he certainly made sustained and systematic attempts, by persuasion and propaganda, to inject life into the predominantly passive and conservative mercantile communities of Riga, Narva and Reval; in accordance with his relatively liberal mercantilism he lowered and simplified tolls; he provided better harbours and better seamarks; he resolved the ancient rivalry between Reval and Narva; he continued the hopeless attempt to annex the trade of Archangel; and he struck the first blow against the mercantile predominance of the Dutch by the Customs Ordinance of 1645.[2] But none of these things had much relevance to the struggle for a victorious peace in Germany; and it was that struggle which for Oxenstierna was the decisive issue.

It may be conceded, however, that with the end of the German war the angle of vision shifted. Sweden had now to maintain and defend her empire without the help of foreign subsidies, without 'contributions', and with small prospect (in peace-time) of increased parliamentary grants. Much now depended on tolls and customs and indirect revenues. It had always been Axel Oxenstierna's policy to commute, pawn or sell the standing revenues of the crown for lump sums, on the argument that the old revenues in kind were less useful to an imperial power than revenues in cash, and that the passing of crown lands into private hands would mean increased productivity, which would in the long run benefit the fisc. He looked forward to an expanding income from indirect taxes. And the massive alienations of crown lands after the coming of peace (partly to discharge obligations which could be discharged in no other way) made the increase in indirect revenues more vital than ever. It was in these

---

[1] Arnold Soom, 'Die merkantilistische Wirtschaftspolitik Schwedens und die baltische Städte im 17. Jahrhundert', *Jahrbücher für Geschichte Osteuropas* 1963, p. 183.

[2] *Ibid.*, pp. 193–5. The Customs Ordinance of 1645 is printed in A. A. von Stiernman, *Samling utaf Kongl. Bref, Stadgar och Förordningar angående Sweriges Rikes Commerce, Politie och Oeconomie i Gemen*, II (Stockholm 1750), pp. 400–14. For Oxenstierna's economic ideas, see e.g. *AOSB* I.xiv.290; xv.458. For an example of his moderate and flexible approach to tariffs, see K. R. Melander, *Die Beziehungen Lübecks zu Schweden und Verhandlungen dieser beiden Staaten wegen des russischen Handels über Reval und Narva während der Jahre 1643–1653* (Helsingfors 1903), pp. 42, 50, 53, 58.

circumstances that Oxenstierna produced in 1651 his *Instruction* to the newly-established College of Commerce; and here for the first time, it might seem, we do get a real blueprint for something resembling the Svensson–Attman model, in that Oxenstierna laid it down that it must be Sweden's objective to obtain a monopoly of the whole trade of the Baltic, and as far as possible to carry it in her own ships.[1]

But not until after the peace, and only as a consequence of the peace, was it possible to formulate such a programme as this. It is noteworthy that when in 1644 Oxenstierna first put forward the suggestion for a College of Commerce he did so in terms of the purely administrative improvements which might be expected to result from it, and had no word to say of the grand commercial perspectives upon which he dilated so eloquently seven years later. The same had been true of Lars Grubbe's *Promemoria* of 1637, and of Daniel Behme's project of 1649.[2] And certainly it was not a programme for further imperial expansion: it was rather an exhortation to draw the maximum commercial advantage from the empire which had already been acquired: like Johan Risingh, who analysed the imperial economic problem in the fifties, Oxenstierna believed that without effective control of its trade the empire would be 'a lifeless body'.[3] The attempt to implement a programme of expansion was left to Charles X. There is no need to qualify any of the reasons which have already been put forward to explain Charles's violent and restless activity: they were certainly operative, and they were essentially political. But the cost of his enterprises presented formidable problems. Mobilization, and initial campaigns, had to be carried out on credit. The seizure of the Vistula delta thus became a first priority – not because of any long-term notion of trade monopoly, but simply because the licences were immediately indispensable to the war-chest: in the prolonged Council-debates of December 1654, when the reasons for arming were exhaustively discussed, considerations of commercial strategy are scarcely so much as men-

[1] Stiernman, *Samling utaf Bref...angående...Commerce*, ii, pp. 669–76 prints the *Instruction*: for the College of Commerce see Sven Gerentz, *Kommerskollegium och näringslivet* (Stockholm 1951).
[2] *RRP* xii.498 (9 April 1644).
[3] For Risingh's ideas see Ellen Fries, 'Johan Classon Risingh', *HT* 1896.

tioned; though Gustaf Bonde did rather grudgingly concede that 'it would be no bad thing if we could get hold of Danzig'.[1] But in the attack on Denmark in 1658 it is undoubtedly true that economic and political motives were fused into one: on the one hand the political dream of an empire of Scandinavia (once attributed to Gustav Adolf); but on the other the blinding inspiration that if Denmark were conquered, if the Sound passed into Swedish hands, there would be no need to worry about licences in Livonia, Prussia, Pomerania or Mecklenburg: with far less effort and expense, Sweden could more than make them good by levying tolls at the Sound.[2] The conquest of Denmark would realize simultaneously Charles X's Scandinavian imperialism, and Oxenstierna's visions of controlling the trade of the Baltic; and the Sound Tolls would provide the wherewithal to maintain a fleet strong enough to defy the indignation of the trading nations of the West, and above all of the Dutch.

Charles' death put an end to these dreams for decades to come. The Regents, and after them Charles XI, were indeed concerned (as any government must be) to develop trade in their dominions: the trade of Narva and Reval, in particular; but also of Stade. In 1669 Magnus Gabriel de la Gardie drafted a list of possible concessions to Dutch and English traders, to be offered in return for an undertaking to abandon the trade by Archangel, and deal instead through Reval, Narva and Nyen.[3] But Swedish agents now reported pessimistically on the prospects of diverting trade from Archangel.[4] Least of all could it be said of the Regents that they took Svensson as their model for foreign policy. For that foreign policy was only in a limited degree positive and dynamic. Essentially, it was a continuous attempt to adapt Sweden's measures to her resources, and to look dignified at someone else's expense. The dream of monopolizing the Russia trade perhaps

[1] *RRP* XVI.2–36: Bonde's remark is on p. 28.

[2] Hans Villius, 'Operation Sjaelland augusti 1658', *Scandia* 1953–4; Birgitta Odén, 'Karl X Gustaf och det andra danska kriget', *Scandia* 1961. One of Sweden's objectives when negotiating the peace of Roskilde had been to acquire the area north of Trondheim, including the copper mines at Røros, Løkken and Kvikne; and Charles also revived the Arctic policy of Charles IX, in the hope of getting possession of Vardøhus, and thereby controlling the sea-route to Archangel: *ibid.*, pp. 88–94.

[3] P. Weiselgren (ed.), *De la Gardieska Archivet*, XII (Lund 1839), pp. 84–6.

[4] Nyström, 'Mercatura Ruthenica', p. 287.

persisted in the terms of Johan Gyllenstierna's Danish treaty of
1680, though the importance of this element in it has been
disputed.[1] But after 1681 Sweden's alliance with the Dutch made
any serious renewal of economic imperialism unlikely.

Charles XII, too, might fairly claim that his foreign policy was
wished on him by his enemies. Its political objectives and
motivations are sufficiently obvious; but it has also been shown
that he was not unaffected by economic considerations.[2] This, it
must be confessed, does not seem to me to be a revelation
calculated to stagger conservative historians, or compel a re-
adjustment of perspectives. However, it is certainly true that in
1701 he diverted the trade of Kurland ports to Riga; and that in
1703 he did what no other Swedish king did – established an
effective control of Danzig. And in 1705, when he concluded the
peace of Warsaw with Augustus II, he inserted economic
provisions designed to give Sweden and her provinces a grip on
the trade which flowed down the Düna, and provide better
security for Riga's access to her economic upland. But, one may
well ask, what else was to be expected of an impecunious monarch
at the height of his military power? Finding himself in a position
to extort advantages of this kind, he extorted them – as Gustav
Adolf had not been able to do in 1617. But from this it is a far
cry to proving that it was in order to obtain such advantages that
he had crossed the Düna in the first place.

In a quite different context Georg Landberg once uttered a
salutary warning to all pioneers of New Schools. 'The man who
demolishes one myth', he wrote, 'is himself inevitably to some
extent the creator of another. If he fails to realize that fact, if he
believes that he is a kind of superior, objective New Broom in
the historical workshop, then the new myth assumes a dangerous
character.'[3] It may be that in this case the danger is not unduly
great. For if we look at the matter dispassionately, the controversy
between the Old School and the New resolves itself into a single
question: did Sweden seek for increased customs revenues in order

[1] Landberg, *Johan Gyllenstiernas nordiska förbundspolitik*, pp. 109ff.

[2] Jerker Rosén, *Det karolinska skedet* (Lund 1963), pp. 314–15, 326; Karl-Gustaf
Hildebrand, 'Ekonomiska syften i svensk expansionspolitik, 1700–1709', *KFÅ* 1949.

[3] Georg Landberg, 'Den svenska stormakten på sin middagshöjd 1648–1697',
Nordisk tidskrift 1951, p. 8.

to finance campaigns which had a political motivation; or were the campaigns launched essentially in the hope of acquiring the vastly increased revenues which could be expected from a monopoly of the trade of the Baltic, and especially the trade to Russia? No single answer fits all the facts; and perhaps it is not of ultimate importance what the answer is. For whichever theory we prefer, each presupposes, as the motive behind Swedish expansion, a feeling in her statesmen of insecurity and weakness: political weakness, in the one case; and in the other an economic inadequacy which must be remedied if the state were ever to be safe. But if I must record my own impression, it is that as far as I know it the evidence for the 'economic' theory strikes me as sparse at many of the points where one might expect to find it most abundant. In the correspondence of Gustav Adolf and Axel Oxenstierna, in the Propositions to the Diet, in the debates of the Council and the Estate of Nobility, a man will look a long time before he amasses any sizeable dossier to support it.

Nevertheless, though opinions may vary as to the strength of the economic motive as a determinant of policy, there can be no two opinions upon one thing: namely, that from start to finish the Swedish imperial adventure was accompanied by a never-ending struggle to find the money to finance it. In the next chapter I shall discuss how well Sweden was adapted – socially, politically, constitutionally – to become an imperial power, and to maintain her status when that had been accomplished. And not the least of the factors I shall have to consider is that economic hair-shirt which the Swedes never ceased to hug to their bosoms, and which became the national boast to offset much that was amiss, or the standard deprecation to excuse it: 'Swedish poverty'. It is with Swedish poverty, then, that the next chapter will initially be concerned.

II

Resources, Material and Moral

SUCH, then, was the imperial superstructure which necessity or ambition, economic design or political calculation, imposed upon the Swedish realm.

How far was that realm qualified to sustain the burdens and responsibilities laid upon it? What natural advantages, what special aptitudes had it at its command, to fit it for its imperial destiny?

At first sight, one would be tempted to pronounce those advantages few and insufficient. Sweden was, and until the nineteenth century would remain, a poor country: sparsely populated; underdeveloped; the victim of a rigorous climate. In Gustav Adolf's reign Sweden and Finland together had a population of perhaps a million and a quarter. That population did indeed increase throughout the century; but the annual rate of growth was very slow: somewhere between 2.2 and 2.7 per thousand.[1] Perhaps the land could hardly feed many more: men were well content with an average harvest yield of fourfold, or sixfold on the best land; between 1523 and 1781 only one year in eight could be reckoned a good one: in the northern half of the country the eating of bark-bread was almost a normal resource, and the cows were dry for nine months of the year.[2] Domestic production of grain was barely sufficient in ordinary times, and in a few years left a surplus for export. The Brandenburg statesman Count Waldeck once declared 'The Swedes are a hungry people, and hence they are dangerous and hard-hearted.'[3]

[1] Bertil Boëthius, *Gruvornas, hyttornas och hamrarnas folk. Bergshanteringens arbetare från medeltiden till gustavianska tiden* (Stockholm 1951), pp. 11–12.

[2] N. Keyland, *Svensk allmogeskost* (Stockholm 1919), II, pp. 10, 112–16; E. W. Dahlgren, *Louis de Geer, 1587–1652. Hans lif och verk* (Uppsala 1923), I, pp. 312–15; Bertil Boëthius and Eli F. Heckscher, *Svensk handelsstatistik 1637–1737* (Stockholm 1939), pp. 104–5.

[3] Quoted in Ellen Fries, *Erik Oxenstierna. Biografisk studie* (Stockholm 1889), p. 217.

43

They may well have been better nourished than the average
French peasant or Polish serf – hence perhaps the incredibly rosy
picture of the condition of the Swedish peasantry painted by
Charles Ogier[1] – but like him they fell easy victims to harvest-
failure and pestilence: in Sweden, as in France, there were years
of demographic disaster: 1648–50, 1696–7, 1709–11. Even in the
best of times, it might have been supposed that the struggle to
wring a living from a grudging nature would leave little
manpower to spare for overseas conquests. The great wars
brought with them casualties which Sweden could not easily
replace. Certainly the German war – in this respect, as in so many
others – marked a turning-point: for an enterprise of this
magnitude and duration the old resources were inadequate. As
Svante Sparre told the Estate of Nobility in 1650, former wars
had been minor affairs, 'but the German war has been of a
different nature; it has needed more men, more ammunition,
greater amounts of pay, for which our old revenues would not
suffice'.[2] In 1632 Sweden had some 175,000 men in the field. How
could she hope to provide and maintain such a force?

The plain answer is that she could not. In fact the great
enlargements of Swedish territories were won by armies consisting
mainly of mercenaries: at Breitenfeld the Swedes totalled 20.2%
of the army; at Lützen 18%;[3] and the percentage steadily declined
thereafter. The native soldiers were carefully hoarded and husbanded because they were so precious, were given garrison duties,
set to hold points of vital importance against the day when defeat
in battle, or a mutiny of mercenaries, would make it imperative
to have reliable troops in strategic places. The system persisted to
the end of the Thirty Years War, though in the very last year of
that war a draft of 7,000 was sent over from Sweden; but this was
by that time unusual.[4] It was the system upon which Charles X
also relied. But it was obviously inappropriate to the kind of
defensive war, fought within Sweden's borders, which Charles XI
had to fight against Denmark; and the ordinary militia-levies had

---

[1] See *Från Sveriges storhetstid*, ed. and trans. S. Hallberg, p. 21. But other foreigners
made similar observations.

[2] *SRARP*, IV$_2$.430 (15 October 1650).

[3] Sven Lundkvist, 'Svensk krigsfinansiering 1630–1635', *HT* 1966, p. 384.

[4] Försvarsstaben, *Från Femern och Jankow till Westfaliska freden* (Stockholm 1948),
p. 295.

then to be supplemented by mercenary soldiers recruited in
Sweden itself, sometimes by violent methods.[1] The military
reforms of Charles XI in the eighties were designed to safeguard
the country against another emergency of this sort, as well as to
reduce as far as possible its reliance upon foreign soldiers of
fortune. His creation of a large, automatically self-recruiting
national standing army largely solved this particular problem, and
by its very success ensured that his son should employ another
method than the old. It therefore happened that Charles XII's wars
differed from all the wars since 1630, in that they were fought
by armies which were mainly composed of native troops. And
that was one reason why they were felt to be uniquely burdensome:
in 1700 Sweden and Finland raised no less than 100,000 men; by
1708 the number had risen to 111,000, which represents a figure
of something like 5% of the total population.[2] Professor Åström
calculates that the Österbotten regiment, permanently stationed
at Riga, must have taken every tenth adult male in the province.[3]
Yet the number of casualties after 1700 was far less than used to
be thought; the old story that at the end of Charles's reign the
Swedish forces were composed of old men and boys is now
discredited. It was the famines and plagues of 1710–11, rather than
the war, that caused a temporary upset in the established
demographic pattern. But it seems certainly to be true that the
end of the war in 1721 left the nobility, at any rate, with a
significant excess of females;[4] and the exhausting effort required
to defend the empire (to say nothing of the attempt to conquer
Russia) with armies made up of native troops alone, was felt, and
rightly felt, to be greater than Sweden could sustain for very long.

[1] *SRARP* XII.330 (23 February 1678) for the Nobility's complaints on this score. For
the remarkable resourcefulness and flexibility of procedures employed to meet this crisis
– procedures which had well learned the lessons of the Thirty Years War and its system
of 'contributions', and which in another aspect looked forward to the devices whereby
Charles XII was later to supplement his standing army of provincial regiments – see
the recent study of Berndt Fredriksson, *Försvarets finansiering. Svensk krigsekonomi under
skånska kriget 1675–79* (Stockholm 1975).
[2] Stig Backman, '*Karl XII och den ryska sjömakten, av Arnold Munthe. Kritisk
granskning av del I*', *KFÅ* 1927, p. 157.
[3] Sven-Erik Åström, 'The Swedish Economy and Sweden's Role as a Great Power
1632–1697', in *Sweden's Age of Greatness*, p. 64.
[4] In 1721 there were five women to three men of marriageable age in the Estate
of Nobility: Sten Carlsson, *Bonde – Präst – Ämbetsman: Svensk ståndscirkulation från 1680
till våra dagar* (Stockholm 1962), p. 32.

But if the wars were to be carried on mainly by mercenaries (as was in fact the case between 1630 and 1675) one may well ask how Sweden could afford to pay them, for mercenaries (especially cavalry) were extremely expensive. And Sweden in the period of expansion really was a poor country, and not only in regard to manpower. Foreign travellers in the first half of the century found its buildings mean, its standards of living low (except in the matter of drink), its nobility deficient in the elegances, or even the comforts, of civilized life, its church sunk in apostolic poverty. Only by a great national effort and a Dutch loan (never repaid)[1] had it been possible to pay off Älvsborg's ransom. A middle class, as England or Holland knew it, was only slowly beginning to form: very few wealthy native merchants or *entrepreneurs*; virtually no professional middle class at all. Sweden's statesmen complained that apart from Stockholm the country had no real towns; and they pursued a policy of town-founding, apparently under the impression that the country would thereby grow rich. It was an impression which speedily proved to be mistaken. The new towns for the most part remained mere fishing villages: Gabriel Oxenstierna in a moment of disillusionment called them 'thieves' kitchens'.[2] But if the burgher lived meanly, so did his colleagues in the first and second Estates. The parson on his stony glebe, the petty noble who was too often a scarcely-presentable squireen, were often hardly to be distinguished from the surrounding peasantry. At meetings of the *riksdag* members of the Nobility would be excused attendance on grounds of poverty; Charles IX found it necessary to warn them

[1] E. W. Dahlgren, *Louis de Geer*, I, pp. 74–92: cf. Axel Oxenstierna's cynical comment in *AOSB* I.xi₂.738.

[2] For Oxenstierna's view of the new towns see Nils Ahnlund, *Axel Oxenstierna intill Gustav Adolfs död* (Stockholm 1940), pp. 228–9. And see Eli F. Heckscher, 'Den ekonomiska innebörden av 1500-och 1600-talens svenska stadsgrundningar', *HT* 1923, pp. 324–5, 341; Birger Steckzén, *Umeå stads historia 1588–1888* (Umeå 1922), pp. 31–7. The official view appears from the Proposition to the *riksdag* of 1641: 'That this realm's broad acres are so little cultivated, developed and improved, is the result not so much of the cold, the rocks and the mountains (for these too have their conveniences), but mostly because our way of life is not according to the customs of other civil nations, which are embodied in sober regulations and definite rules, but is rather directed to solitude, self-will and each man's presumed convenience, than to a formed society and collective existence. Wherefore there is no great kingdom, nay, hardly any good-sized principality in the world which has fewer (and worse) towns than Sweden': *SRARP* III.168.

not to allow their servants to attend his coronation in ragged clothes; and when in 1632 it was proposed that the first Estate should send a deputation to Germany to congratulate Gustav Adolf on his victories, the proposal ran into difficulties because most of the members were said to be too poor to contribute, and they were afraid the mission would have a mean appearance in German eyes.[1]

In the early 1620s the ordinary revenues brought in an amount equal to perhaps 1.5 million silver *dalers*. A modest sum; though perhaps adequate to peace-time needs. But between 1600 and 1660 there was not a year when Sweden was not at war, and the ordinary revenues rarely sufficed. From time to time recurring financial crises produced humiliating and bizarre effects: important embassies could not start for lack of money, the court would be hard put to it to find cash for food and firing, wages of crown servants would go unpaid for long periods, there would be proposals to cut down the number of schools.[2] The soldiers of the greatest military power in Europe would desert by dozens to save themselves from starvation, and the Council would debate the possibility of hiring out Sweden's armies in order to escape having to pay them.[3] The need to finance continental campaigns drove the government to a war-economy based on money rather than goods, and led it to sell or pawn the revenues of the crown in return for lump sums in cash; with the result that by the mid-fifties perhaps as much as three-fifths of the ordinary revenue had passed into private hands, and two-thirds of the country's fiscal units had become exempt from taxation.[4] This was a situation which entailed grave difficulties once the wars were over; and it led directly to the *reduktion*. But nevertheless it remains true that in the period of imperial expansion Sweden never found herself in really disastrous financial difficulties of the type which plagued (e.g.) France and Spain. The crown was never reduced

---

[1] *SRARP* I.189; II.47–8.

[2] E.g. *SRARP* IV.625 (20 December 1651); Georg Wittrock, *Karl XI:s förmyndares finanspolitik*, I (Uppsala 1914), p. 76; Carlson, *Sveriges historia*, II, pp. 293–5. For the desperate expedients proposed in 1710 (which included selling the national trophies, and commandeering church bells) see *SRARP* XVIII.16, 19, 114, 121, 285–6.

[3] Wittrock, *Karl XI:s förmyndares finanspolitik*, I, pp. 133, 304, 343, 413; II, p. 182.

[4] For a clear account of the problem of liquidity and the implications of a war-economy, see Åström, 'The Swedish Economy'.

to selling honours;[1] after 1600 there was no significant debasement of the coinage; and before the period of Görtz's siege-economy the government did not resort to the printing-press. In almost every major country in Europe the strain of war produced a financial crisis, which in turn led to a constitutional crisis, and in many cases to the popular disturbances and insurrections of the mid-century. In so far as Sweden was affected by this crisis at all, the constitutional implications were muted, and the state extricated itself with apparent ease, and without internal disorder. The finances were certainly strained on occasion – from 1613 to 1619, from 1629 to 1631, from 1655 to 1661. But the worst crises came after the process of empire-building was complete: it was the Regents for Charles XI who first began the bad habit of anticipating revenue. Before Pultava, the burden of taxation was probably heaviest, and the salaries of civil servants worst paid, in the period of disaster and reconstruction which extended from 1675 to 1689. But the state was never bankrupt, or near it; at least, in war-time. Until Charles XI's reign the debt was surprisingly modest, and vigorous efforts were made to pay it off: in 1644 it was estimated to have been not more than a million d.s.m.; between 1661 and 1668 Gustaf Bonde's economical administration reduced it from 10.5 to 3.5 millions;[2] between 1680 and 1693 the ruthless measures of Charles XI brought it down from 40 millions to 19, and simultaneously carried through a comprehensive programme of rearmament. As Professor Åström pertinently remarks, 'In comparison with other absolute monarchies in the early modern period of European financial history, the Swedish *régime* did take a rather different attitude to its creditors, whether native or foreign'.[3] The nearest Sweden came to a 'bankruptcy' on the Spanish model was Charles XI's forced conversion with retroactive effect.[4] It was a principle of the constitution that the king should 'live of his own', on his ordinary revenue, and

---

[1] A possible exception is the Regency's ennoblement of Joel Ekman (Gripenstierna) in 1669, in return for a substantial loan: Wittrock, *Karl XI:s förmyndares finanspolitik*, II, p. 167; Arne Munthe, *Joel Gripenstierna: en storfinansiär från Karl XI:s tid* (Uppsala 1941), pp. 45–6.

[2] C. T. Odhner, *Sveriges inre historia under Drottning Christinas förmyndare* (Stockholm 1865), p. 134; Carlson, *Sveriges historia*, IV, pp. 277, 378.

[3] Åström, 'The Swedish Economy', p. 92.

[4] Carlson, *Sveriges historia*, IV, p. 301.

Charles XI by the end of his reign was actually doing so. That revenue had to be supplemented, of course, by extraordinary grants in war-time; but such grants were always forthcoming. In peace-time it was not so easy. And by an apparent paradox to which I shall return, it was just in peace-time that the burden of empire was most heavily felt, and was least able to be sustained.

On the whole, then, the state was solvent. And it had at its disposal a number of splendid assets. It did, indeed, initially lack the capital to develop them; but it offered so attractive a field for investment that this was scarcely a problem. For the first two-thirds of the century not the least important of Sweden's imports was capitalists: men from the Low Countries or Germany who came to Sweden attracted by the tempting privileges offered by the crown, by the rich metallurgical resources of the country, by cheap labour, abundant water-power, vast supplies of fuel, and by the fact that the effects of the European price-revolution were here muted and delayed. These men – de Geer, the de Besches, Rademacher, the Mommas, to name only a few of them – were responsible for a remarkable efflorescence of Swedish mining and its associated industries. The enormously rich copper mine at Falun was 'Sweden's Indies', and in the second quarter of the century it had what was virtually a European monopoly: its only competitor was Japanese copper, imported by the Dutch. The *régale* upon copper yielded revenues which in the 1620s were of crucial importance in paying for Gustav Adolf's wars. And when, in the decades after 1650, the productivity of Falun declined, copper's place was more than supplied by iron. From the second half of the century onwards the high-quality Uppland ore, the so-called 'Oreground iron', commanded the European markets, as it would continue to do until late in the eighteenth century: Sweden thus became for a time the world's biggest producer of copper and iron; and incidentally became self-sufficient in the matter of armaments – no inconsiderable advantage. And the fact that despite the adjustments necessitated by the wars Sweden remained throughout the century to an unusual extent a natural rather than a money economy meant that the impact of the price revolution, and the social strains which attended it elsewhere, were here only lightly felt. Thanks to the demand for her copper and iron, moreover, she was able to escape the full severity of the general slump which set in after 1620, and of the secular depression of the latter half of the century. Under a protective commercial policy, and in response to the impulse provided by flourishing industry, she secured after 1660 an increasingly considerable share of Baltic freights. Though it is difficult to credit Aksel Christensen's statement that by 1648 the Swedish mercantile marine had become 'fully able to compete with the Dutch fleet trading to the Baltic',[1] the Swedish equivalent to a Navigation Act, promulgated in 1645, certainly had stimulating effects; and the second and third Anglo-Dutch wars presented opportunities which Swedish shipowners were not slow to seize.[2] Throughout the first half of the century Sweden had benefited from a situation in which her exports rose in price considerably faster than her imports.[3] Despite the burden of war, and the heavier burden of peace, the country was getting steadily richer. The living-standards of the nobility, and after them of the non-noble civil servants and merchants, had by 1660 moved up towards the level that was usual on the continent. Already in 1654 Axel Oxenstierna had tartly remarked that a noble who was too poor to attend the *riksdag* was fit only to be a peasant;[4] and in the following four decades absence on the plea of poverty is noticeably rarer than it had been in the 1630s.[5] If so much of the crown's revenue had not been alienated between 1640 and 1655 we should more easily have noticed that it was, in fact, buoyant: in 1632 the annual loss of

[1] Aksel Christensen, *Dutch Trade to the Baltic about 1600. Studies in the Sound Toll Register and Dutch Shipping Records* (Copenhagen 1941), p. 98.

[2] Birger Fahlborg, 'Ett blad ur den svenska handelsflottans historia (1660–1675)', *HT* 1923, *passim*.

[3] Eli F. Heckscher, *Sveriges ekonomiska historia från Gustav Vasa* (Stockholm 1936), I, p. 225.

[4] *SRARP* VI.260 (15 June 1654).

[5] At the Stockholm *riksdag* of 1660 no members of the Nobility pleaded poverty as an excuse for absence; in 1668, though occasionally new members were admitted without making a contribution to *Riddarhus*-funds, it was held that a fine of 50 *daler* was too small to deter wilful absentees: *SRARP* VIII.288; X.364, 556. Of the 68 new members admitted to the House of Nobility in 1686, only five were excused a contribution on the ground of poverty; of 87 admitted in 1689 only two; of 109 in 1693 only two – and this despite the *reduktion*: *SRARP* XV.123–6, 365–8; XVI.66–70. In July 1675 M. G. de la Gardie, admitting that there was much poverty, explained characteristically that 'poverty comes of *luxu* in clothes and entertainment among the burghers here [in Stockholm], which is so great that those from Riga and Stralsund who see it are astonished that it is permitted': C. Adlersparre, *Historiska samlingar* (Stockholm 1812), p. 149.

revenue in respect of farms officially described (for fiscal purposes) as 'desolate' amounted to 262,000 silver *daler*; by 1669 the figure had dropped to 69,000.[1] New colonization of the waste brought substantial increases of revenue – so substantial, that a recent estimate puts them at 'considerably in excess' of that which Gustav Vasa in his day had obtained from the confiscated church lands.[2] The customs, farmed out for 63,000 *rdr* a year till 1634, were by 1641 yielding 312,000.[3]

Nevertheless, it remains true that even when these things have been taken into account, and even when it is conceded that in the period after 1660 the upper Swedish nobility could bear comparison, for baroque extravagance of living, with their compeers in other lands, the state's resources, human and material, remained inadequate to the country's political commitments. Foreign visitors to Sweden in the seventies were impressed by the architectural splendours of Stockholm – Magalotti even considered that its buildings were unmatched outside Italy;[4] but it was symptomatic that the triumphal arches which Jean de la Vallée erected in Stockholm for Christina were made of nothing more solid than wood, canvas and plaster;[5] and in 1671 a Danish traveller noted that the monument to Descartes, being also of wood, was 'for the most part destroyed by time and rain'.[6] At the end of the century the total annual value of Swedish foreign trade per head of the population was only about 16p; while that of England was seven times as much;[7] and Heckscher estimated Sweden's annual expenditure at 6.3 million *d.s.m.*, England's at 16.8 million, and France's at 88 million.[8] Despite the emergence of substantial native capitalists, their financial solidity was still dangerously dependent on Dutch backing: the Momma-Reenstierna brothers, for instance, who owned an enormous

[1] Carlson, *Sveriges historia*, II, p. 11 *n* 2.
[2] A. S. Kalvemark, reviewing Lars-Olof Larsson, *Kolonisation och befolkningsutveckling i det svenska agrarsamhället 1500–1600* (Lund 1972), in *HT* 1973, p. 113.
[3] Boëthius and Heckscher, *Svensk handelsstatistik 1637–1737*, pp. xvii–xxiv; and *cf.* Odhner, *Sveriges inre historia*, pp. 239–40; and Carlson, *Sveriges historia*, v, p. 102.
[4] Lorenzo Magalotti, *Sverige under år 1672* (Stockholm 1912), p. 9.
[5] M. A. Ohlsson, *Stormaktstidens privatpalats i Stockholm* (Stockholm 1951), pp. 17–21.
[6] Corfitz Braem, *Dagbok under en resa i Sverige åren 1671 och 1672* (Stockholm 1916), p. 29.
[7] Boëthius and Heckscher, *Svensk handelsstatistik 1637–1737*, pp. xlviii–ix.
[8] Eli F. Heckscher, *Ekonomi och historia* (Stockholm 1922), p. 99 *n* 1.

complex of enterprises stretching from Lappland to Ösel, crashed in the 1670s because the Dutch war deprived them of capital support from Holland, and the Swedish state was in no position to repay its debts to them.[1] Domestic resources, in fact, were still inadequate to great imperial policies, as they had been from the beginning; and because they were inadequate, methods had had to be devised, at an early stage, to supplement or replace them. These devices were used with such success that Sweden was able, at least until the empire had taken its final form in 1660, to undertake without undue strain enormously expensive and protracted military efforts.

The basic principle was formulated by Gustav Adolf in 1623, when he wrote to Oxenstierna: 'if we cannot say *bellum se ipsum alit*, I see no way out of what we are engaged in'.[2] The war must pay for itself; which meant that it must be paid for by enemies, allies or neutrals – by anyone, in short, other than Sweden. In the years between 1630 and 1648 the principle was applied with unswerving logic and astonishing success. Neutrals were mulcted of duties at the Baltic ports which had passed into Sweden's possession. Subsidies from France and the Dutch, though relatively insignificant in amount, helped to tide Sweden over critical moments. But the main source of supply was Germany itself. By enormous exactions in cash and kind from occupied allied or enemy territories, or from cities prepared to buy their safety, the needs of the armies were handsomely provided for. In the good years after Breitenfeld Germany contributed annually to the Swedish armies a sum which Lundkvist estimated at as much as ten or twelve times the amount of Sweden's ordinary budget.[3] A carefully devised and equitably applied system of 'contributions' was graded according to ability to pay; and since 'contributions' were paid in cash, and the money was usually spent in the area from which it was extracted, the system inflicted less damage on the economic life of Germany than might have been expected: indeed, it depended for its success upon the preservation

---

[1] For the meteoric rise and disastrous collapse of the Momma-Reenstiernas, see Per Sondén, 'Bröderna Momma-Reenstierna. Ett bidrag till den svenska handelns och industriens historia på 1600-talet', *HT* 1911.
[2] *AOSB* II.i.398, Gustav Adolf to Axel Oxenstierna, 1 April 1628.
[3] Sven Lundkvist, 'Svensk krigsfinansiering 1630–1635', *HT* 1966, p. 410.

of a reasonable measure of local prosperity.[1] The immediate impact of these procedures upon the Swedish Exchequer was startling: in 1630 the Swedish taxpayer had to find 2,800,000 silver *daler* for the German war; by 1633 the amount he had to contribute had dropped to 128,000.[2] Well might Axel Oxenstierna write to his brother in 1636: 'our forefathers and we have never carried on any war with greater ease to ourselves...than this one'.[3] As long as the League of Heilbronn lasted, Oxenstierna pursued a successful policy of shifting purely Swedish debts on to the shoulders of other League members; and he availed himself of Sweden's *jus belli* to give vast donations of territory (conquered or to be conquered) to military *entrepreneurs* in return for large advances.[4] To borrow Roland Nordlund's phrase, it was 'war by proxy'; and very lucrative the method proved, as long as it lasted. Not that the Swedish taxpayer was not called upon for considerable sums. The German war might more or less support itself, but Sweden had to find the money for the defence of the Baltic provinces, for the navy, for garrisons, and for those armaments which were made at home. But by the closing years of the war these accounted for at most 35% of the total budget of the state; and of that budget not more than 4% went to the struggle in Germany.[5]

The system of course had its limitations. It required that Sweden be victorious, that her allies be faithful to her, that there should be large tracts of rich occupied territory available for exploitation. After Nördlingen, and especially after the Peace of

[1] For this question of war finance, see Lundkvist, 'Svensk krigsfinansiering'; Klaus-Richard Böhme, 'Geld für die schwedische Armeen nach 1640', *Scandia* 1967; id., *Bremisch-verdische Staatsfinanzen 1645–76* (Uppsala 1967); Per Sörensson, *Krisen vid de svenska armeerna i Tyskland efter Banérs död* (Stockholm 1931), pp. 101–36; Gun Cliff, 'Kring finansiering av ett svenskt stormaktskrig', Kungl. Livrustkammaren, *Historiska bilder* II (Stockholm 1949), pp. 91–111; Försvarsstaben, *Från Femern och Jankow till Westfaliska freden*, pp. 69–91; Hans Landberg, Lars Ekholm, Roland Nordlund, Sven A. Nilsson, *Det kontinentala krigets ekonomi. Studier i krigsfinansiering under svensk stormaktstid* (Uppsala 1971); Sune Lundgren, *Johan Adler Salvius. Problem kring freden, krigsekonomien och maktkampen* (Lund 1945), pp. 212–15.
[2] Lundkvist, 'Svensk krigsfinansiering', p. 385.
[3] *AOSB* I.xv.534, Axel Oxenstierna to Gabriel Gustafsson Oxenstierna, 18 June 1636; and cf. ibid. I.viii, 610 (to Sten Bielke, 9 May 1633).
[4] Roland Nordlund, *Krig genom ombud. De svenska krigsfinanserna och Heilbronnförbundet 1633* (Uppsala 1974).
[5] Försvarsstaben, *Från Femern och Jankow till Westfaliska freden*, p. 91.

Prague, these preconditions increasingly ceased to exist; and Sweden found herself, stripped of her German allies, fighting with her back to the sea in Pomerania and Mecklenburg. It was then that the French subsidies became valuable, enabling the recruitment of new troops, a break-out from the narrow Baltic base, the overrunning once more of enemy territory, and a renewal of the system of contributions. As long as Sweden continued to win victories she could count on winning them at little cost to herself. Retreat and defeat upset the financial equation. Peace destroyed it.

Charles X found this out when he launched the next stage of expansion in 1655. In contrast with Gustav Adolf, he started with no war-taxes in his pocket. He could look forward to no subsidies from allies. The Swedish native army, now reduced to a peace-time establishment of about 50,000, could not carry out the task alone. His revenue from 'licences' was much below the level of 1630. The method of financing the war which he proposed to himself was in all essentials that which had served so well in the past: contributions from occupied territory, tolls on the Vistula. But he had to face the huge initial cost of recruiting, transporting and fitting out his armies: there must be an interval of months before contributions could begin to come in, and before the trade of neutrals could provide a significant yield. The partial *reduktion* of 1655, one of whose objects was precisely to provide money for the army, was equally slow in making its effect. His only resource, then, was to wage war on credit. By borrowing from native nobles and financiers, by making concessions in the matter of the *reduktion* to men such as Königsmarck who had emerged from the war bloated with Queen Christina's donations, by giving bills at several months' date, by raiding the civil list, by postponing full payment of the troops he levied, he contrived to prime the pump and establish the situation from which victories could be expected to flow, and the necessary revenues to flow after them.[1] If Charles X had been as methodical a strategist as his uncle, they might have flowed according to plan – not as freely, perhaps, as of old, for Poland was not so rich a country as Germany – but

[1] Hans Landberg, *Krig på kredit. Svensk rustningsfinansiering våren 1655* (Stockholm 1969); id., *Statsfinans och kungamakt. Karl X Gustav inför polska kriget* (Stockholm 1969); Klaus-Richard Böhme, *Bremisch-verdische Staatsfinanzen*, p. 203, for the loans from Königsmarck.

still perhaps in sufficient quantity to pay his armies. As to his creditors, he might reasonably expect to satisfy them as so many creditors had been satisfied in the past, with donations of occupied territory. In the event, the calculation proved unsound. The Polish war did not pay for itself, and left no pickings to satisfy creditors; the attempt to overwhelm Denmark and seize the Sound Dues (which would have solved the financial problem) miscarried; and Charles X on his death left a debt of over 10 million.[1] But on an annual budget of 2.5 million, at the close of sixty years of warfare, this could hardly be said to be a crushing burden, and indeed Gustaf Bonde succeeded by rigid economy in paying off 7 millions of it in five years. Thus 'Swedish poverty' interposed no serious obstacle to the fulfilment of Sweden's bloody destiny. Thanks to the system of contributions Sweden was able without undue strain to effect the empire's acquisition. It would prove a much harder task to pay for its preservation. In 1660 the period of expansion seemed to have come to an end: for forty years Sweden rested upon her arms. But when at last Sweden's enemies rashly pressed the button which set Charles XII in motion, when the victor of Narva resumed the imperial advance, the old techniques still seemed the best; and Lithuania and Poland found themselves subjected to contributions as well-organized and carefully calculated as those which had served so well in the Thirty Years War.[2]

By proxy or on credit, then, Sweden was able to provide the men and the money without which her conquests would not have been possible. But it is obvious that men and money by themselves were not enough: they might avert defeat; they could not ensure victory. In the last resort the empire rested on Sweden's military superiority to her enemies; and that superiority derived from innovations and practices which for a couple of generations gave Sweden a clear advantage over all competitors. There is no need to enter into a detailed description of them: it is sufficient to note

---

[1] For Charles X's difficulties in supporting his armies after the peace of Roskilde, and the necessity for transferring them to foreign soil, see his letters to Matthias Biörenklou, printed in C. Adlersparre, *Historiska Samlingar*, v (Stockholm 1822), pp. 177–214.

[2] Sven Grauers, 'Den karolinska fälthärens underhåll 1700–1703', *KFÅ* 1968, pp. 124–34; *id.*, 'Den karolinska fälthärens underhåll 1704–1707', *KFÅ* 1969, pp. 126–4.

that Gustav Adolf, improving on the linear tactics of Maurice of Orange, produced a solution – perhaps as good a solution as the technologies of his age permitted – to the perennial problem of combining fire-power, flexibility and defensive strength. The Swedish conscript militia became for a time the most advanced and formidable military instrument in Europe; and in due course the mercenary forces which soon came to form the bulk of the Swedish armies learned the new methods from Swedish drill-masters. The period from 1632 to 1648 might be dominated numerically by mercenary troops; but the purely native element in the Swedish armies was always an indispensable *corps d'élite*. The Form of Government of 1634 placed the native standing army upon a permanent establishment; and that army acquired a justified self-confidence, a tradition of victory, comparable to that which had once carried the Spanish *tercios* through many a desperate situation. To the very end it remained a psychological asset of incalculable importance: without that asset, some of the more spectacular achievements of the wars of Charles X and Charles XII would scarcely have been possible.[1] Even the capitulation of Perevolotchna did not finally extinguish it, as Magnus Stenbock was to demonstrate. It was reinforced, of course, by the military genius of the long succession of first-rate soldiers which Sweden had at her disposal. And the fact that successive kings were commanders-in-chief in reality, and not only in name, went far to ensure unity of command, integrated strategies, and a tolerably satisfactory level of performance in the supply-services.

The victories of the Swedish armies did not rest only on tactical innovations, or the ability of their commanders. They presupposed also an efficient administrative machine. And among the things which made it possible for Sweden to become a great power was, in fact, the creation of an administration of unusual strength, continuity and honesty. This showed very clearly in the precise and orderly methods of the College of War, where 'not only every gun and every pike, but every spade and every cannonball was carefully noted down and accounted for, in strong contrast to the waste and disorder of many of the German states'.[2] The

---

[1] This point is strongly made by Artéus: Gunnar Artéus, *Karolinsk och europeisk stridstaktik 1700–1712* (Göteborg 1972), pp. 128–30.

[2] Birger Steckzén, in conversation with the author, February 1949.

creation of the College of War was however only one facet of
the great work of reorganization which had filled much of the
reign of Gustav Adolf: in 1644 Axel Oxenstierna, looking back
to the state of affairs which had existed when first he became a
member of the Council, contrasted the order and method which
the great king had introduced with the confusion prevalent in the
time of Charles IX.[1] The process of reform was already apparent
in the remarkably efficient measures taken to collect the final
instalment of Älvsborg's ransom;[2] it was codified in the Form of
Government of 1634, which, whatever else it was or was not (still
a matter of sharp controversy) was above all an administrative
statute. Its reorganization of the central government into five
Colleges, its careful delimitation of function, its prescription of
methods of procedure, provided the administrative base upon
which the great war was fought. The administrative structure it
set up caught the attention, and extorted the admiration, of
European observers, and it was to provide the model for similar
administrative reforms elsewhere – most notably, in Russia.

We can see now that the admiration of contemporaries was a
little excessive. The system often functioned less well than its
originators had expected. It did not impose a satisfactory system-
atization on the management of the finances: for that Sweden
had to await the reforms of Charles XI. The machinery for
periodical examination of the work of the Colleges never established itself, and its failure to do so was sharply censured by critics
of the Regents for Christina.[3] There was bitter inter-collegiate
rivalry on occasion: for the whole of Charles XI's minority the
Chancery and the Treasury conducted an unedifying and
damaging feud. There was at first a lack of trained personnel,
aggravated by absenteeism, laziness or malingering among some
of the members.[4] The method of collective decisions by a board
probably blunted the incisiveness of executive action. The chiefs

[1] 'The Chancellor remarked how confusedly matters were ordered in King Charles's
time, and afterwards in the first years of the late king, and how the late king worked
to get the Colleges in their *esse*, as also that the Diets might be orderly conducted':
RRP x.680 (12 December 1644).
[2] Sven Lundkvist, 'Rörlighet och social struktur i 1610-talets Sverige', *HT* 1974,
p. 209.
[3] *SRARP* III.409–16; and *cf.* Odhner, *Sveriges inre historia*, pp. 125–6.
[4] Oxenstierna in 1637 observed that Sweden could out-fight the Danes, but the
Danes, having better-trained personnel, would always out-negotiate the Swedes: *RRP*
VII.304.

of the Colleges – the five great officers of state for those established
by the Form of Government of 1634; for those added subsequently,
their presidents – were until the coming of the absolutism invariably drawn from the narrow, exclusive circle of members of
the Council of State; which meant in practice from the highest
level of the aristocracy. This could entail serious disadvantages.
Since the range of choice for the highest posts was so narrow,
members of the Council could move from one office to another
without having acquired, or indeed having had the time to
acquire, the specialized *expertise* which the office demanded. Their
senior subordinates – the vice-presidents, the permanent civil
servants who corresponded to under-secretaries of state – did
indeed very quickly become a highly-trained body of expert
administrators; but before 1680 they were not always able to
compensate for a chief who was more or less of an ignorant
amateur. Seventeenth-century Sweden seems to have shared with
eighteenth-century England a robust belief in the ability of its
aristocracy, by mere circumstance of birth, to shoulder the burden
of office and discharge the business of government, whatever the
nature of that business might be. In the last half of the sixteenth
century, when they had claimed a monopoly of high office on
the ground that they alone were fitted to bear it, their claim had
had some substance; for as a class they were then better qualified
than any other to serve the state, and their claim was a claim for
good governance. It was also, in a constitutional point of view,
a preferable alternative to what was termed 'the rule of secretaries'
– the rule, that is, of unscrupulous, able, low-born careerists,
responsible only to the king whose agents they were. But by the
middle of the seventeenth century it was no longer possible to
defend aristocratic monopoly on grounds such as these. It is true
that in certain areas this lofty amateur approach was much less
noticeable than in others: the College of War was from the
beginning in the hands of the professionals, and here *expertise*
extended to the very top. For almost the whole century the
Chancery – which was, after all, the real *anima regni* – was dominated by Chancellors who held office for long periods (in Axel
Oxenstierna's case, for more than forty years), and were for the
most part very well fitted to hold it. But the system could quite
easily produce a president of one of the Supreme Courts whose

knowledge of procedure was slender and whose command of the law questionable. The evils of aristocratic monopoly of the highest office were seen most plainly, perhaps, in the Admiralty, where the *riksamiral* could by no means be counted on to know his business; so that, as Ulf Sjödell has recently pointed out, from the mid-thirties to the mid-seventies the Admiralty was in a condition of more or less permanent crisis, against which knowledgeable subordinate officials struggled in vain.[1] Not until the coming of the absolutism after 1680 placed that arch-bureaucrat Charles XI in effective control of the bureaucracy were these and similar abuses firmly tackled, and merit could supplant birth and status even at the highest levels. But with all its drawbacks the Swedish administrative system, as it was laid down in 1634 and as it expanded thereafter, was a carefully planned and relatively sophisticated machine, which looked modern in comparison with the antique confusions to be found elsewhere. Some of the defects tended to vanish in course of time; notably the lack of trained personnel, which was one aspect of Sweden's educational backwardness. It was remedied by a change in educational fashions: young men began to aspire to the civil service who would before have read theology; and by the fifties the supply of qualified candidates exceeded the demand.[2] Already by the 1660s Sweden was well on the way to that closely-knit, well-organized class of government officials which was to dominate the state until the moment came when an absolute king sought to undermine them, and himself perished in the resulting ruins. The bureaucracy expanded to meet the increasing range and complexity of the state's business;[3] but business increased so quickly that officialdom probably grew thinner on the ground as the Age of Greatness progressed. Most of the Colleges had their own intake of trainees, and in the case of one of them – the Supreme Court – the trainee system had effects which extended far beyond immediate departmental concerns. For the 'auscultators', as its trainees were called, got jobs in all branches of the civil service, local as well

[1] Ulf Sjödell, *Riksråd och kungliga råd. Rådskarriären 1602–1718* (Lund 1975), pp. 45–9, 51, 53–6.

[2] Sven Edlund, *M. G. de la Gardies inrikespolitiska program 1655* (Lund 1954), pp. 31–2.

[3] And not, perhaps, as David Gaunt puts it, to 'control' its subjects: David Gaunt, *Utbildning till statens tjänst. En kollektivbiografi av stormaktstidens hovrättsauskultanter* (Uppsala 1975), p. 98.

as central, – hence the anxiety of the Nobility that more of their members should be employed in that capacity[1] – and disseminated throughout the service a training in the law, and a respect for legality; and thus gave a reinforcement, from a quarter where such reinforcement might not always have been expected, to the deeply-ingrained Swedish belief in the rule of law. They had a devotion to the crown and the crown's interests which saved them from the political attitudes of the French *parlements* or the Inns of Court; but unlike the local civil servants in some other countries they were never primarily, by training or inclination, the agents of the fisc.[2] Finally, though there were fierce attacks in the 1650s on the fees and *douceurs* extorted by the secretaries of state, the civil service had the very rare advantage that it was not venal: in seventeenth-century Sweden the sale of offices simply did not occur. Nevertheless, for all its merits, the system functioned too deliberately to cope successfully with a major crisis. The new administrative methods devised by Charles XII at Timurtasch, the new short-cuts which were characteristic of Görtz's direction of affairs, must make it at least questionable whether the administrative structure laid down by the Form of Government of 1634 was adequate to an imperial power under siege, though it had served well enough before the siege was formed, and would resume its tranquil efficiency once it had been lifted.

The Swedish army, and the Swedish civil service, were thus at the heart of the Swedish imperial state, as they were later to be at the heart of the Austro-Hungarian empire. And we may pause to ask how far, as a consequence of half a century of continuous warfare, Sweden was a militarized society. The question is easier to ask than to answer. Geijer, in his day, had no doubt what the answer would be: the military spirit, he wrote, suffused the whole of Swedish society.[3] That the army counted for much in that society can hardly be denied. The army officers, for instance, were separately represented at the *riksdag*, though they never acquired the full status of an Estate, and though their influence in practice seems to have been very small. When in Charles XI's time society was elaborately stratified by the Table of Ranks, the army men

---

[1] See *SRARP* XIV.204: grievances of the Nobility, 1682.
[2] Gaunt, *Utbildning till statens tjänst, passim*, and pp. 31–2, 56–7.
[3] E. G. Geijer, *Det svenska folkets historia* (new edn. Malmö 1928), III, p. 21.

came out at levels which seem disproportionately high in comparison with their civilian compeers. The dominant class in the state, the nobility, saw its duty or its opportunity in military service: in 1626 it was said that 'the greatest part of the nobility are out of the kingdom';[1] in 1710 provincial governors were reporting that the entire nobility of their provinces were either fighting, or prisoners of war, or aged,[2] though this may well be an exaggeration, since the provincial governors were concerned to paint as dark a picture as possible of conditions in their own provinces. The device of the Nobility as a class was after all '*Arte et Marte*', and it has been said that *Riddarhuset* was in effect a sermon in stone upon that text.[3] When in 1625 Gustav Adolf was asking for means to create a standing army he argued that it would provide the nobility with 500 jobs; and Oxenstierna later estimated the number of military and civil posts reserved to them at 800 – which represents a very high proportion of their total male adults.[4] At the *riksdag* of 1693, of 499 nobles present, 248 held military appointments, 176 civilian posts, and only 75 were not office-holders.[5] The military had great social prestige; and no doubt many another young woman of the aristocracy besides that tiresome creature Agneta Horn despised civilian suitors, and set her heart on a '*brav soldat*'. A militarist ethos undoubtedly existed in the aristocracy; though even there it was not perhaps as universally diffused as Geijer imagined. No doubt it is true that in peace-time the officer-class, left stranded by demobilization, sighed for the good old days of brisk action and the prospect of booty.[6] It is clear that a majority, and probably a large majority, of the nobility looked to a military rather than a civil career, if

[1] *AOSB* ii.iii.98, Gabriel Gustafsson Oxenstierna to Axel Oxenstierna, 3 September 1626.   [2] *SRARP* xvii.5–6 (2 April 1710).

[3] Lars Gustafsson, 'Den litterate adelsmannen i den äldre stormaktstidens litteratur', *Lychnos* 1959, p. 31.

[4] W. Sjöstrand, *Grunddragen av den militära undervisningens uppkomst- och utvecklingshistoria i Sverige till år 1792* (Uppsala 1941), pp. 155–6.

[5] *SRARP* xvi.151–64.

[6] In February 1651 Arvid Forbus wrote to his stepson Göran Horn: 'The times are now grown so dear, that there is almost nothing to be got, now the war is over...There be many now who are out of service, whom once the war nourished...Since there is now (glory be to God) peace in all quarters, a man must find his resource in God and his book': Elof Tegnér, *Svenska bilder från sextonhundratalet* (Stockholm 1896), p. 108.

they aspired to be anything more than country gentlemen. It has recently been suggested[1] that in the case of the lesser nobility one reason for this may be that they felt themselves at a disadvantage, owing to their lack of the necessary educational qualifications, when competing for posts in the civil service against members of the higher nobility, and also against university-trained commoners. But Ulf Sjödell has shown that those members of the high nobility who opted for a civil career had a better chance of rising to a seat on the Council than those who went into the army, and still more than the small numbers who entered the navy.[2] Over the whole century some 60% of the members of the Council are estimated to have followed a purely civil career; but in those periods when the political dominance of the high aristocracy was most marked (the regencies for Christina and Charles XI) only six soldiers entered the Council, as against twenty-six civilians; and though for the whole century 40% of Council members were military men, this figure is inflated by the special circumstance of Christina's rewarding the great commanders of the Thirty Years War, and by other accidental circumstances after 1680. Certainly it was not the soldiers who ran the Swedish state: Axel Oxenstierna, Johan Skytte, Johann Kasimir, Per Brahe, Erik Oxenstierna, Herman Fleming, Gustav Bonde, Magnus Gabriel de la Gardie, Johan Gyllenstierna, Erik Lindschöld, Bengt Oxenstierna – there is not a single professional soldier in the list until we come to Arvid Horn; though Axel Oxenstierna and de la Gardie did command armies on occasion. When the wars were over, the great commanders tended to be quietly relegated to governorships of the overseas provinces – positions for which their military talents naturally qualified them – and remained for the most part without much influence at the centre of power in Stockholm.[3]

One of the most conspicuous features of the seventeenth-century Swedish state was the great expansion of the apparatus of government, and especially of the central government. Another was an unusual measure of social mobility. The two things were closely connected. A classic pattern of social advance was peasant–parson–civil servant–nobleman; a cycle which might take three generations or more in the first half of the century, but which

---

[1] Ulf Sjödell, '"Det gamla Lågfrälset" och 1600-talsbyråkratien', HT 1974.
[2] Sjödell, Riksråd och kungliga råd, passim, for what follows.
[3] Though to this generalization C. G. Wrangel was a conspicuous exception.

tended to accelerate after 1680. Since noble competition in the army was strong, men of non-noble origin saw their best prospect of advancement in the service of the state at home. It was the civilians, in fact, not the soldiers, who constituted the mobile and dynamic element in society. The great generals might on occasion reach the supreme eminence of the Council, and having attained it might find themselves employed in a variety of civil offices for which they might be dubiously qualified; but the ordinary noble who served in the army did not thereby much improve his chance of permanent enrichment or enhanced social status: for him, as for his non-noble competitors, the prospects were better if he had a university education which fitted him to follow the civilian line. The wars, through the increasing complexity of the administrative and financial machinery required in order to conduct them, opened the way to new types of men: to financiers and merchants, foreign at first, native later on; to *entrepreneurs* and industrialists; to bureaucrats. The new Supreme Courts and the increasing professionalization of the law, the growth of the universities, fostered the emergence of a previously almost non-existent professional class. The importance of the clergy as the state's unpaid agents, the fact that the Swedish church had virtually no pluralists, produced a clerical population more influential and more numerous than might have been expected – a population either self-recruiting or recruited from below; and despite the brimstone sermons and Old Testament exhortations of its clergy, they were too closely linked, economically and socially, to the congregations to whom they ministered, for them to have much sympathy for any conceivable military *élite*. As to their parishioners, though they might fight valiantly at Breitenfeld or Narva, they had little taste in general for the soldier's life: in April 1655 a member of the Council wrote a memorandum on possible means 'to animate our youth to the profession of arms, which the ordinary man much abhors', and ten years later Clas Rålamb was lamenting that nothing seemed to have been done about it.[1] There were complaints by the clergy that Charles XI's education was too purely military.[2] On the whole, then, it seems likely that the

---

[1] [Clas Rålamb], *Memorial* in *Den svenska fatburen*, no. 7 (4 July 1769), pp. 105–9.

[2] C. Adlersparre, *Historiska Samlingar*, IV (Stockholm 1812), pp. 131–2, which prints the Council debates on a sermon in this sense delivered by the pastor of St Jakob, Stockholm.

martial appearance of Swedish society in the Age of Greatness is something of an illusion. Despite the gloomy predictions of Bishop Rudbeckius, buttressed by examples from imperial Rome, the swollen armies never constituted a danger to the state.[1] Despite the prestige and social advantages of the military, they never dominated society: the civil servants were too strong for that. And above all they were never able, by their own strength or in association with the crown, to undermine the solid constitutional bases upon which the state reposed.

So far, we have been considering the economic and human resources which Sweden had at her disposal for the creation and maintenance of her position as a great power. But it may be questioned whether these assets by themselves would have sufficed, if they had not been supplemented by others, more difficult to measure, but not less real. Empires are not made only by money and manpower. Behind the splendour of sixteenth-century Spain, as behind the emergent Dutch Republic and the rise of Elizabethan England, lay powerful intangible moral forces. The *tercios* did not dominate the battlefields of Europe, Leiden was not defended, nor the Armada defeated, only in virtue of a superior tactic or a longer purse. How was it with Sweden in this regard? What moral capital had she to draw on, to meet the new experiences to which she was exposed?

Certainly one of the things which made it easier to pursue the path of empire was the fact that Swedish society was unusually solid and stable. It was bound firmly together by the tough cement of the Swedish church; it enjoyed the rare blessing of total religious unity.[2] Sweden was the Lutheran Spain. The church encompassed the whole of society, from the monarch and the Council of State to the cottar, pedlar and cowherd. It welded them together by unanimity in doctrine, a reasonable uniformity

---

[1] *RRP* v.293 (10 November 1635).

[2] To this generalization Ingria, with its population mainly Greek Orthodox, was the only exception. By about 1620 Swedish theologians had agreed that the Orthodox were Christians differing only on *adiaphora*; but vigorous though fruitless attempts at conversion persisted until the end of the forties. They were resumed in the 1680s, with a policy of concentrating only on Finnish-speakers (as against Russian-speakers) – a policy which degenerated into real persecution until, on protests from Moscow, it was stopped by Charles XI: Alvin Isberg, *Svensk segregations- och konversionspolitik i Ingermanland 1617–1704* (Uppsala 1973). For the Swedish church in general in this period, see M. Roberts, 'The Swedish Church in the Age of Greatness', in *Sweden's Age of Greatness*, ch. 4.

in observance, common participation in the democratic organs of parochial self-government, and a common obligation to master the catechism. And it was conscious of its responsibility as a unifying agent: Elaus Terserus might consider it his duty to lecture his rebellious parishioners on the social necessity of a privileged nobility;[1] but on the other hand the Estate of Clergy, with Archbishop Lenaeus at its head, in 1650 fought a successful battle to secure the statutory limitation of labour-services. And as the government of the church was democratic at the parochial level, so too the structure of local government rested upon a democratic base. The peasant not only participated in national decisions at the meetings of the *riksdag*, he was also in his native county directly and vitally engaged in the judicial and administrative decisions of the *häradsting*. But it was also a society, as we have seen, which offered opportunities for social advancement: though it can hardly be said that the ordinary soldier carried a baton in his knapsack, the intelligent peasant boy who managed to scrape a university education might begin the ascent of the social ladder by way of the church; the burgher's son who entered the civil service might make a solid career for himself; and by the time that the absolutism had put a premium upon efficiency the son of a blacksmith, or a parish priest, or even a peasant, might end his life as a count or baron.[2] The result was a society which succeeded in escaping some of the afflictions of less fortunate lands: after the 1620s there was for the rest of the century no revolt or civil disturbance of the slightest consequence, except in the former Danish provinces. In a century when almost every major power was called upon to deal with popular revolts, Sweden escaped scot-free. Whatever may have been the case with other countries, it could hardly be asserted of Sweden that her rulers embarked upon wars as a vent for the evil humours of society: there was neither a *noblesse frondante* nor the threat of *croquants* and *nu-pieds* to suggest the expediency of such a bloodletting.[3] Charles X did not undertake his Polish war to distract the minds of the nobility from the *reduktion*: on the contrary, the *reduktion* was seen as a

---

[1] Roberts, *Gustavus Adolphus*, I, p. 122.

[2] See the illuminating list of examples given by Professor Åström, 'The Swedish Economy', p. 78.

[3] For an exception to this generalization see the remarks of Bengt Oxenstierna, quoted in Carlson, *Sveriges historia*, II, p. 117 *n* I (I May 1664).

necessary condition for a necessary foreign policy. The Burghers, among whom a movement of political opposition might on general principles have been considered most likely to emerge, were for long the weakest of the four Estates.[1] They were heavily dependent on the crown to uphold their privileges; their municipal finances were often in such poor shape that they asked the crown to appoint 'royal' burgomasters, since they found the burden of paying their own magistrates too onerous; apart from Stockholm their numbers were insignificant; and they were divided among themselves by local jealousies and clashing economic interests. As to the peasantry, in contrast with (e.g.) Brandenburg, the country's greatness was not founded *ab initio* upon a system of social oppression. The monarchy was not bribed to condone serfdom in exchange for the promise of noble support.

Yet on the other hand it was one of Sweden's strengths that in this period monarchy and nobility laid aside their old rivalry, and went forward together hand in hand. That achievement had been Gustav Adolf's work; and though in the thirties and forties there were moments when the alliance came under strain, it held fast. When Charles XI imposed his *reduktion*, therefore, the result was a situation which was abnormal; and the monarchy tried to remedy it (with a great measure of success) by raising up a new, civil-service nobility to take the place of the old as its ally. The closeness of the relationship between the nobility and the crown was one reason why the first Estate showed a unique readiness to make sacrifices and waive privileges in the name of patriotism.[2]

[1] See Stellan Dahlgren, 'Estates and Classes', in *Sweden's Age of Greatness*, pp. 110ff.

[2] The Council debates in 1636 provide illustrations (and qualifications) of this generalization.

(a) '*The Chancellor:* If the crown has not peasants enough to keep the war going, then the nobility's peasants must give a hand: what the crown lacks we must supply...Above all things we must take the line that Her Majesty and the country are to be preserved, but on the other hand that the Nobility are not to be ruined.

The Marshal: The crown's welfare is our welfare...

The Steward: If the state is in danger, I am less interested in preserving my privileges than in defending the country.'

(b) '*Count Per Brahe:* In no country are there *nobiles* who contribute so much to the crown as the nobility here in Sweden. We do so much, and have done it for so long, that we shall soon have no liberty left.

The Chancellor: That is mere presumption. You think it is liberty if you are free to give nothing to the preservation of the crown. *Vera libertas fundatur super salutem reipublicae...*': RRP VI.536, 661 (13 August, 20 October 1636).

But Gustav Adolf's emollient achievement did not shake another and much older political tradition: the tradition of the common interest of king and peasant in the face of an overmighty aristocracy which threatened at once to undermine the historic freedom of the Swedish commonalty and to reduce the monarch to the position of elective president of an aristocratic confraternity. The alliance of crown and peasantry had been used by Eric XIV to strike down possible dynastic rivals; very recently it had been unscrupulously exploited by Charles IX to effect a dynastic revolution and the judicial murder of his leading noble adversaries. The king was still the supreme court of appeal, and in common parlance 'to go to the King' expressed the belief of the commonalty that though the royal bailiffs might be oppressive, the royal courts accessible to influence from consanguineous nobles, still the sovereign in the last resort could be relied upon to uphold the poor man's cause. No matter that he often enough let them down and quashed their complaints, the peasantry still believed that the king was their friend and ally: at the very worst, better one king than many. So the crown stood between nobility and peasantry, linked by strong ties to each, and neither would willingly risk the loss of its alliance. The peasantry's fear of the nobility, and the clash of Estates which resulted from that fear, aborted any common constitutional front against the crown. This was the situation which Queen Christina was to exploit, with cynical virtuosity, in 1650. It was this central position which Charles XI was forced to evacuate when he pushed through the *reduktion*.

The question remains, however, to what extent this relatively integrated society could be enlisted behind a war effort so demanding and so protracted. How far can the wars be said to have reflected popular feeling? It is certainly true that the hatred of Denmark, stretching back to the days of Engelbrekt and the Bloodbath of Stockholm, and greatly reinforced by the sufferings of the War of Kalmar, was a fact of politics. No doubt it was blunted in some frontier areas by a long-standing tradition of local truces, and by the fact that the Småland uplands looked to ports in Blekinge or Skåne as their natural export routes: the novels of Vilhelm Moberg do reflect something of the truth, even though the reflection is perhaps distorted. Nevertheless, the hatred and fear of Denmark was both deep-rooted and long-lived. Per Wieselgren, whose edition of the De la Gardie Archives conferred an onerous blessing on posterity, has an extraordinary story, drawn from his own experience, to the effect that even at the beginning of the nineteenth century the Småland peasantry were disposed to believe that the Danes were really were-wolves.[1] And if hatred of the Dane was a national feeling, so too was fear of the Russian, especially in Finland. A recent study of how Swedes viewed their eastern neighbours in Gustav Adolf's time[2] reveals that the stereotype of the Muscovite was an insolent, treacherous barbarian, whose Christianity was at least doubtful, whose morals were deplorable, who was individually contemptible, but alarming by reason of his overwhelming numbers: it seems to have been in 1615 that someone for the first time in an official document used the expression 'our old hereditary enemy, the Russian'[3] As to the war with Poland, and the intervention in Germany, the case is less clear; and it is difficult to see why the average Swede should feel deeply engaged in either, except upon the single ground of religion. But by the mid-thirties Oxenstierna no longer considered that religion was a main issue in the German war;[4] and one may doubt whether the confessional zeal of the ordinary man was running very high by 1648. Indeed, it is clear that long before then the Swedish people had to be nerved by systematic and intensive propaganda to make the sacrifices which the state demanded of them. In royal utterances, public proclamations, messages to the Estates, reports to the Council, there is a marked similarity in the characterization of Sweden's enemies. In contrast with Axel Oxenstierna's stereotype of Swedes as

---

[1] *Dela Gardieska Archivet* xv (1841), pp. 34–41. In Charles XI's time Samuel Columbus could write: 'It is an evil thing, a wild and dreadful phantom, around whose skull a hundred serpents writhe, a mere devilish troll: its name is Envy, and these many years it has dwelt for the most part in Copenhagen': quoted in Axel Strindberg, *Bondenöd och stormaktsdröm* (Stockholm 1937), p. 292.

[2] Kari Tarkiainen, '*Vår Gamble Arffiende Ryssen*'. *Synen på Ryssland i Sverige 1595–1621 och andra studier kring den svenska Rysslandsbilden från tidigare stormaktstid* (Uppsala 1974). Cf. *AOSB* I.ii.371, where Axel Oxenstierna writes: 'Est bestia unius et plurimum capitum, vivere sueta suo more, lest sich nicht leichtlich merken undt handeltt niemals sincere, gehett mitt ihren tractaten ob insolentiam langsamb um...'

[3] Tarkiainen, '*Vår Gamble Arffiende Ryssen*', p. 25. And *cf.* Magnus Gabriel de la Gardie on the ineradicable mendacity of the Russians: *SRARP* IX.142 (13 July 1664).

[4] E.g. *AOSB* I.viii.610 (9 May 1633); *RRP* VII.53 (17 May 1637).

simple credulous souls liable to be led by the nose by any crafty negotiator,[1] Danes, Muscovites, Papists generally, were all, it seems, persons who habitually broke faith and harboured sinister designs against the Swedish state: it was so that Gustav Adolf spoke of the Russians after Stolbova; or Oxenstierna when he laid it down that no peace with the Imperialists was possible except when they were under Sweden's foot, with a knife at their throat; or Charles X in 1658, adducing Danish breach of faith for his second attack upon Copenhagen; or Charles XII in 1706, when he rejected any suggestion of compromise with so faithless a monarch as Augustus II. It was a sadly consistent record of human turpitude with which Sweden had to struggle.

It is, in fact, perfectly plain that the rulers of Sweden devoted great care to cultivating public opinion, both at home and abroad. In the years before the intervention in Germany; in 1658 and 1659; in the years after 1700, very great efforts were made to create a favourable climate of opinion in Europe.[2] Success was not wanting, as those familiar with Puritan notions on foreign policy will remember. Even more important was the success at home. Here kings had propaganda-agents ready to their hands: the clergy. As the unpaid local agents of government, as the communicators of all official information to their flocks through the medium of the pulpit, they were the natural vehicles to choose: did not Gustav Adolf, in his farewell speech of 1630, advert to their ability to 'twist and turn the hearts of their congregations'? On the Polish and German issues, at all events, they could be trusted to represent the issue as a struggle between light and darkness, Protestantism and Popery, a struggle in which the peacemakers were to be accounted anything but blessed. The Swedish church had good authority for bringing 'not peace, but a sword'; and the sword it brought was the sword of the Lord and of Gideon. Their spirit was that of the Old Testament; their

---

[1] *AOSB* I.xiii.349.

[2] Sverker Arnoldsson, *Krigspropagandan i Sverige före trettioåriga kriget* (Göteborg 1941); Göran Rystad, *Kriegsnachrichten und Propaganda während des dreissigjährigen Krieges* (Lund 1960); Arne Stade, 'Gustaf Horn och Nördlingenkatastrofen 1634', *HT* 1965; Helge Almquist, 'Bidrag till kännedomen om den karolinska tidens politiska publicistik', *HT* 1936; Sven Olsson, *Olof Hermelin, En karolinsk kulturpersonlighet och statsman* (Lund 1953); Jerker Rosén, 'Diplomatiens organisation och metoder under det stora nordiska kriget', in Rosén, *Från Sveriges stormaktstid* (Stockholm 1966), pp. 170–81.

psalms were psalms of battle and of hate; and though they waited in vain for the day when they could sing that Babylon the Great is fallen, they could celebrate Swedish victories by the psalmody of vengeance.[1] Sweden's godly armies were well supplied with chaplains to the forces, some of whom were later to rise to positions of authority within the church, and such men, coming home with the smell of powder still in their nostrils, could be relied upon to exhort their congregations and denounce the dark designs of Rome. Rudbeckius compared Gustav Adolf with Judas Maccabaeus; and more than a decade before Cromwell's New Model Army Botvidi was telling the troops that they were 'God's Israel, the true Israelites'.[2] Administratively, the clergy played a great part in the country's mobilization for war; psychologically, a still greater, in nerving their flocks to sacrifice by strong doses of selected truths.

It seems likely that this type of propaganda was beginning to wear thin by the end of the Thirty Years War; and in the wars of Charles XI and Charles XII it was inappropriate. As to Charles X, the nature and impact of domestic propaganda still awaits examination: he dragged the country into war, first with Poland, then with Denmark, and at last with a European coalition of the most heterogeneous religious complexion; and none of these wars would appear to have been popular. Abroad, indeed, enthusiasts such as Drabik and Comenius contrived to see him as a resurrected Lion of the North, as once they had seen Gustav Adolf; but the fable of the Lion of the North, though it had been disseminated in Sweden for propaganda purposes in the years before 1630, had thereafter been mainly for export.[3] Its place was taken in Sweden by another myth, equally long-lived, equally bizarre, and much more potent. This was the mythical–historical fantasy of the Ancient Goths. It is impossible within a small compass to do justice to the extraordinary ramifications of this theory, but in essential outline it maintained that Sweden was the oldest of the nations,

[1] E. Liedgren, *Svensk psalm och andlig visa* (Uppsala 1926), pp. 144–5; *cf.* Botvidi's report, *SRARP* 1.156–7.

[2] Ingvar Kalm, *Studier i svensk predikan under 1600-talets första hälft* (Uppsala 1948), pp. 191, 195.

[3] J. Nordström, *De yverbornes ö* (Stockholm 1934), ch. 1. The notion of Charles XII as the Lion was revived, however, in an attempt to improve morale after Pultava: Strindberg, *Bondenöd och stormaktsdröm*, p. 373.

having been founded soon after the Flood by Magog, the son of Japhet. The people of Magog's realm had been too far away from Babel to be involved in the confusion of tongues which was the consequence of that enterprise; and hence they had retained what was in effect the original language of mankind, the language in which God spoke to man. From their original settlement around Uppsala they had spread widely over the face of the earth. They had conquered Asia Minor, they had taken imperial Rome; and who could doubt that it was Uppsala which gave its name to the Salic Law? Still earlier, the Swedes had been involved in the siege of Troy; and it was Sweden that was the home of the Amazons. The journeys of the Argonauts had of course taken place in the Baltic; the Pillars of Hercules were located at the Sound; and Sweden was the Hyperborean land, the Isle of the Blest, and (in the final elaboration of the theory) Atlantis. The Goths who dwelt in Sweden (and who derived their name from Magog's son Götar) had indeed been a race of mighty warriors and great conquerors; but they had also been endowed with the ascetic virtues of the ideal heroes of chivalry, and they had made their country the home of a rich and varied culture, centring on the great temple at Uppsala, ringed about with its chain of massy gold. They had taught philosophy to the countrymen of Plato; they had founded the sciences of astronomy and chronology; they had produced a great literature (now, alas, perished) written in those runic characters which were its only visible memorial. And if the runic alphabet itself had been in danger of being forgotten, that was owing to the designing arts of the papacy, which had foisted the Roman alphabet on the world as a convenient vehicle for superstition.[1]

I have conflated earlier and later versions of the theory in an attempt to administer it in one convenient mouthful; but it did, in fact, develop as time went on. Its origins date back at least to the fourteenth or fifteenth centuries. Some of it was borrowed from Spanish historians such as Isidore of Seville, or from Jiménez de Rada's *Historia Gothorum*; much was indigenous. A critical moment occurred at the Council of Basel in 1434, when Bishop

---

[1] Nordström, *De yverbornes ö*, ch. II and pp. 94–152; *id.*, 'Goter och Spanjorer', *Lychnos* 1944–5, pp. 257–75; *id.*, 'Historieromantik och politik under Gustav Adolfs tid', *Lychnos* 1937, *passim*; Strindberg, *Bondenöd och stormaktsdröm*, *passim*.

Ragvaldi of Växjö claimed primacy for Sweden above all other nations, on the ground that it was the oldest. His claim (which the Council disallowed) was repeatedly cited thereafter (in Sweden) as an authority to support the antiquity of the Goths. But the really decisive impact was made by the publication, in 1554, of Johannes Magnus' *Historia Gothorum Sveonumque*, which for the first time provided a full-blown history of each of the long list of the kings of the Ancient Goths. Its influence outside Sweden was appreciable; its influence inside Sweden, enormous. Eric XIV translated it in prison; Charles IX and Gustav Adolf both sponsored official translations into Swedish; Johan Skytte arranged for its translation into German. It formed one of the staple ingredients of Erik Sparre's famous oration of 1594; its echoes sound clearly in Gustav Adolf's farewell speech to the Estates in 1630.[1] There can be no doubt of its influence on Gustav Adolf: his tutors, Johan Skytte and Johannes Bureus (who, incidentally, was the pioneer in the field of runology) were firm believers in Johannes Magnus, and passed on their belief to their pupil; in 1617, on the occasion of his coronation, he appeared in a tournament in the character of King Berik, who had ruled Sweden in the year 836 after the Flood, had been the first king to mount overseas expeditions, and had conquered Poland, Pomerania and Mecklenburg.

There is no space to trace the later developments of the theory. What is important to notice is that it was supported by some of the best minds of this century, and by Swedenborg in the next. Its influence was long-lasting: Charles X in 1658 spoke of leading his Goths to Italy;[2] Gunno Dahlstierna's *Göta kämpavisa* is said to have done much to create the heroic myth of Charles XII;[3] Charles XI, as well as Charles XII, can be considered prime specimens of that austere, chivalric sense of duty which was considered to be one of the attributes of the Gothic hero; and even Queen Christina, with her helm-topped effigies, headlong rides, and epicene sartorial tastes, is not too far from Johannes Messenius' Penthesilea, Queen of the Amazons.

It is possible or probable that the influence of Gothicism was limited to the upper classes and the educated; though it should

---

[1] *SRDA* III.378–82; *SRARP* I.140–1.   [2] Carlson, *Sveriges historia*, I, p. 546.
[3] Strindberg, *Bondenöd och stormaktsdröm*, p. 326.

be noted that a Swedish translation of Bishop Ragvaldi's oration is said to have been a popular chap-book which enjoyed a steady sale at fairs and markets;[1] and it is a fact that the citizens of Kalmar, disliking the idea of a municipal brewery, demanded that they be allowed to brew at home 'according to the liberty of the Ancient Goths'.[2] Successive governments certainly conceived it as part of their duty to sponsor research which would support the theory and confound captious foreign criticism. Gustav Adolf and most of his successors patronized antiquaries: he made Bureus antiquary royal, and in 1629 commissioned him to prepare a sylloge of runic inscriptions. When Skytte endowed the chair of eloquence at Uppsala he laid it down that its holder be bound to deliver orations on the achievements of 'the old Gothic men'. There was a great blossoming of antiquarian studies under the *aegis* of Magnus Gabriel de la Gardie, who promoted the promulgation of what must surely be the first general ordinance for the preservation of ancient monuments, stood patron to Rudbeck's *Atlantica*, and did not hesitate to devote some of the precious French subsidies to financing antiquarian research. In 1679, at a moment of the most desperate economic stringency, Charles XI somehow found the money to put the *Collegium antiquitatis* on a sound financial footing; and nine years later he sent Sparfvenfeldt at the state's expense to unearth relics of the Ancient Goths in Asia Minor.[3] The Swedish nobleman who sent his sons to Italy on the grand tour (which was just beginning to come into fashion) expected their tutor to direct their attention to the old 'Gothic' buildings of Padua and Ravenna:[4] monuments of glories that once had been, and which in this better time should be again. For not the least

---

[1] *Ibid.*, p. 43.

[2] Folke Lindberg, '1619 års stadga om städernas administration', *Svenska stadsförbundets tidskrift* 1937, p. 10.

[3] See Henrik Schück, *Johan Hadorph. Minnesteckning* (Stockholm 1933), pp. 38, 49, 106, 121–2. Sparfvenfeldt's instructions ran: 'As H.M. has an especial desire that all that redounds to the Swedish and Gothic nation from former times may be brought to light, and as it is well known how the Goths and Swedes after their first coming to this country went out again and possessed themselves of new lands and kingdoms both in Asia and Africa, as well as nearer at hand in Europe, and many memorials of them are no doubt to be found in Hungary, Austria, on the Black Sea, in Thrace, Greece, Italy, Switzerland, France and Spain, you are to endeavour to discover whether any documentary evidence of them is to be found there': Carlson, *Sveriges historia*, v, p. 337 *n* 2.   [4] *Erik Dahlbergs dagbok* (pocket edn Stockholm 1962), p. 37.

important element in the Gothic legend was its insistence on a Golden Age in the past, and a strongly implied suggestion that one day that age would come again. The Swedes viewed the creation of their empire with the less astonishment, because to many of them it seemed a return to a long-pretermitted Natural Order.

Now it is of course true that similar fantasies could be found elsewhere in seventeenth-century Europe: in Holland, in Denmark, in France, in Germany, and not least in England, where the Arthurian legend had enjoyed a boom under the Tudors, and Henry VIII could talk of his claim to continental lands on the basis of Arthur's conquests. (Arthur, it is as well to remember, was said to have conquered Russia, Lappland, Norway, Iceland and Greenland – an achievement of almost Gothic dimensions.) Arthur's descent from Brute conferred legitimacy and prestige; precisely as descent from Magog did. England's New Troy on the banks of the Thames is a parallel to Magog's Uppsala. Though Arthurianism exhibited perhaps a less imaginative approach to etymology than Gothicism, it was fully its equal when it came to anagrams: to make 'Charles James Steuart' read 'Claims Arthur's Seat' involved at least a strain, whereas no candid mind could ignore the perfect concordance of 'Gustavus' and 'Augustus'. For Lars Wivallius, Gustav Adolf was Augustus in very truth: he was the hero destined to conquer all nations and establish the rule of peace; through him the reign of Christ should be prepared; and after him would follow Christ's second coming.[1] It was a vision which appropriated to Sweden those ideas of the *translatio* of the mediaeval Empire to the North which had been applied first to Charles V, and subsequently to Francis I and Elizabeth: a *translatio* which should also be a *reformatio*, the coming of the reign of Justice, the return of the Golden Age. And to whom, if not to Queen Christina, the virgin pacificator of Europe, could the famous, evocative line of Vergil be applied: *Jam redit et virgo, redeunt Saturnia regna?*[2] At least it was an identification a good deal less difficult than that undertaken by Sir Richard

---

[1] Birger Lövgren, 'Wivallius som patriotiske siare', *Samlaren* 1912, p. 89.

[2] For a study of these and related ideas see Frances A. Yates, *Astraea. The Imperial Theme in the Sixteenth Century* (London 1975).

Blackmore, who devoted two weighty epics to demonstrating the identity of King Arthur with William III.[1]

But indeed the cases were rather different. Arthurianism in England was born of dynastic needs, and this truth is not weakened by the fact that songs about King Arthur still live on in popular memory. Gothicism had undoubtedly an important propaganda purpose, as a stimulus to morale and national pride, and as an incentive to recover land which the Goths had ruled long ago: the world's great age was to begin anew. But it was more than that. It expressed a widespread popular patriotism. Men believed in it because it fulfilled a psychological as well as a political need: the need to assert the national dignity against an outside world that was economically more affluent, more favoured by nature, culturally richer and more advanced, than the thinly-peopled backward land in the remote recesses of the Baltic; the need to offset present insignificance by the boast of past glories; the need to equip themselves with a great national legend; the need for ancestors. And Gothicism, unlike Arthurianism, had no rival legend to contend with. The Puritan lawyers effectively exploded Arthurianism by setting up the opposing ideal of the Saxons, and by rediscovering the Anglo-Saxon tongue: Arthur was ousted by Alfred. But the comparable progress of runology, and the discovery of the Icelandic sagas, so far from upsetting the Gothic ideal rather complemented and supported it – or at least was made to do so.[2] Thus the Ancient Goths owed their success to the fact that the fabulous story fell on soil which was ready to receive it; and Gothicism, with its absurd challenge to the world outside, made its contribution to the fostering of a nationalist spirit: in this respect (and in this respect only) the dramas of Messenius are akin to Shakespeare's historical plays.

I turn now, finally, to one feature of Swedish society which certainly had direct relevance to Sweden's emergence as a great power: the constitutional situation. It was a remarkable fact,

[1] See R. F. Brinkley, *The Arthurian Legend in the Seventeenth Century* (London 1967), pp. 176–80; Samuel Kliger, *The Goths in England. A Study in Seventeenth and Eighteenth Century Thought* (Cambridge, Mass. 1952).

[2] The Icelandic sagas became known (in Swedish translations) as a result of the capture during Charles X's Danish war of the Icelander Jonas Rugman: Carlson, *Sveriges historia*, II, p. 309; V, p. 322.

significant of the deep-rooted strength of Swedish constitutional traditions, that the stresses generated by the country's imperial expansion did not entail the erosion of her liberties. Political liberties did not begin to be endangered until the empire was clearly on the defensive; and such of them as were lost after 1680 were freely surrendered to Charles XI: it was only under his successor that the Diet could be muzzled by the simple *fiat* of a despot in a Turkish kiosk. In this the Swedish experience contrasts strikingly with the melancholy record of the decline of representative institutions in France, Spain, Brandenburg and the Habsburg lands. At the end of the Age of Greatness, as at its beginning, Sweden remained a parliamentary state.

The *riksdag* was remarkable among representative assemblies in that it included an Estate of Peasants which enjoyed a status and consideration unique in Europe. Its consent to new taxation and to levies of recruits was necessary; and it could not be taken for granted. Though at times attempts were made to bully it, in general it had to be coaxed and persuaded; and its objections and its grievances were often enough supported by the Estate of Clergy, many of whose members had come from peasant homes, and most of whom lived in close touch with their peasant congregations. And if the assent of the Estate of Peasants could not be assumed, neither could that of the Estate of Nobles, since demands for men and money often infringed their privileges.

In regard to foreign affairs the *riksdag* had rights which had either been laid down in Gustav Adolf's Accession Charter of 1611, or rested upon a constructive interpretation of it. They had a right to be consulted before the king made an offensive war, or concluded a peace; it was thought expedient to inform them of important alliances and treaties. And formally the provision of the raw material for foreign policy depended upon parliamentary sanction: new taxes, new levies of men, were *grants*. Though by 1648 the bulk of war-finance might come from Germany, and though the greater part of the armies fighting there might be mercenaries, the right to grant or to refuse did give to the Estates – on paper – a real measure of control. But on the whole they refrained from using it. It was not that their constitutional rights were illusory: it was simply that – with whatever groans and predictions of ruin – they suffered themselves to be persuaded. At

riksdag after *riksdag* it is the same story: the Proposition outlines
the international situation, recounts the progress of the war, and
appeals for more men or money or both. In all four Estates there
is more or less of resistance: the Peasants protest that they are too
heavily burdened to bear any more; the Clergy dilate on the
blessings of peace; the Nobility are troubled at the prospect of a
further erosion of their privileges and exemptions. Deputations
and messages pass to and fro between them; firm stands on
principle are decided on. It is time for Axel Oxenstierna, or Per
Brahe, or Jakob de la Gardie, to intervene. He comes down from
the Council chamber in solemn state; half an hour's pungent but
paternal eloquence to the Nobility, concluding with a sharp
exhortation to put their patriotism before their privileges, is
enough to demolish *their* resistance; and when the Nobility have
thus freely taken upon themselves burdens which they strictly
have no call to bear, with what conscience can the other Estates
persist in trying to evade them? The new tax is accepted, the
government expresses grave satisfaction that a good spirit has
prevailed in the end, and proceeds by way of sugaring the pill to
give sympathetic consideration to some of the less intractable
grievances; after which, in a spirit of at least superficial fraternity
in misfortune, the Resolution of the *riksdag* is cooked up in the
Chancery, and the members are free to go home.

Hence the true importance of the *riksdag* for the development
of the Swedish empire lay not in the fact that it had rights and
privileges which might have checked or delayed that development
if they had been consistently invoked, but rather in the fact that
the *riksdag* was applied to, that it was made an accomplice, and
that this practice induced a feeling of corporate responsibility for
policy, a feeling of participation, which made noble and non-noble
alike more willing to bear the burdens which that policy entailed.
Up to a point, it was an empire made with parliamentary assent.
The crown secured the advantage of something like a national
consensus; but that consensus did not inhibit the free play of *raison
d'état*. The sense of national solidarity in a national cause was
expressed in a dozen Resolutions upon the government's Propositions. It is the implicit assumption behind Gustav Adolf's
farewell speech to the Estates in 1630. But Gustav Adolf was doing
no more than clothe in particularly memorable words a device

of government which remained the ordinary resort throughout the whole period of the wars, and one which Axel Oxenstierna – after some initial scepticism – would also well know how to use.

Yet it was in fact no more than a device: one of those *arcana imperii* about which a wise statesman would take care to be silent. For when it came to foreign policy, on critical occasions the real decision was taken, not by the Estates, not by the Secret Committee (which was concerned with *quomodo* rather than with *an*), not even by the Council, but by the sovereign personally. It is of course true that sovereigns would seek advice from those to whom they gave their confidence, and on occasions might even follow it. Charles IX's views on Denmark may have been reinforced by Nils Chesnecopherus; Gustav Adolf and Axel Oxenstierna undoubtedly proceeded upon a basis of constant and intimate consultation, though it would not be easy to point to many occasions when the chancellor's arguments persuaded the king to change his mind; Charles X's Council in December 1654 gave him the advice which he wanted to hear, and which it was Erik Oxenstierna's business to manoeuvre them into giving, and the section of the Council which he took with him to Germany in 1658 showed a satisfactory readiness to endorse his decision to renew the attack on Denmark. But none of this really made much difference: the Vasas were too self-confident and too imperious to be easily turned aside from their purposes, once they had made up their minds. Eric XIV's agreement with Reval was his personal decision. John III persisted with the campaign in Estonia in defiance of his Council. The Estates disapproved of Charles IX's invasion of Livonia; the Council deplored his provocation of Denmark. The *riksdagsordning* of 1617 expressly gave to the king the right to adopt whichever opinion might seem best to him, in the event of a difference between the Estates; but he never seems to have availed himself of that right, and in regard to foreign policy he did not need to do so. The decision to attack Poland in 1621 was taken, not merely before the *riksdag* was informed of it, but even before the matter had been laid before the Council.[1] The decision to invade Germany was preceded by long-drawn agonized debates in the Council; but they were debates arranged on the pattern of an academic disputation; to

[1] Norberg, *Polen i svensk politik*, p. 114.

some extent they were rigged beforehand; and the king's contributions to the discussion sufficiently indicated on which side his
inclinations lay. The share of Council and *riksdag* in the whole
affair was to provide the king with absolution-in-advance if his
measures should turn out ill. After 1636 it was the same story, with
Oxenstierna in the king's place. Queen Christina began the war
against Bremen in 1653 not only without consulting the *riksdag*,
but without even informing the Council. In the great Council
debates of December 1654 the point was more than once made
that no war was possible without the consent of the Estates; but
when the Estates met a few months later they found that Charles
X, having manoeuvred the Council into acquiescing in the raising
of troops, and having proceeded to recruit them on credit, had
left no financial alternative but to employ them – overseas.[1] The
Regents for Charles XI perhaps provided an exception to this
general pattern; but by that time the empire was already made.
Even so, it was a long time before anything like a serious debate
on foreign policy took place in any of the Estates. In 1658, and
again in 1664, the House of Nobility did indeed discuss foreign
policy, but the discussion was conducted in that artificial style of
a formal academic disputation which the Council knew so well,
and did not really get down to the basic issues.[2] The first real
debate on foreign affairs does not come until 1672;[3] and not until
1675 do we get an extended, full and free expression of opinion
in the Estates.[4] When at last it came, it proved truly explosive;
and the preliminary blasts of 1675 led directly to the great
detonations of the 1680s. Thus, as a result of the government's
tactic of spreading the responsibility by making the *riksdag*
accessories after the fact, the provisions of Gustav Adolf's Accession Charter in this respect remained a dead letter. In regard to
foreign policy the monarchy was as near as makes no matter
absolute, long before 1680. When formal absolutism came, the
best the *riksdag* could hope for was – to be informed. Charles XI

[1] *RRP* xvi.1–36; Hans Landberg, *Krig på kredit. Svensk rustningsfinansiering våren 1655*
(Stockholm 1969); *id.*, 'Kungamaktens emancipation. Statsreglering och militärorgan-
isation under Karl X Gustav och Karl XI', *Scandia* 1969; *id.*, 'Decemberrådslagen 1654.
Karl X Gustaf, rådet och rustningsfrågan', *KFÅ* 1968; Stellan Dahlgren, 'Charles X
and the Constitution', in *Sweden's Age of Greatness*.
[2] *SRARP* vi.301 (21 April 1658); ix.74 (7 June 1664).
[3] *SRARP* xi.146, 150–6.   [4] *SRARP* xii.79, 89 (16, 18 September 1675).

did indeed take care to inform them. But it would never have occurred to his son that the Estates had anything more to do with his decisions than to obey them. Before 1693 the conduct of a war had required the summoning of the Estates;[1] but Charles XII's war continued for ten years, and Charles himself was an exile in Turkey, before a Committee of the Estates was summoned by a nervous Council to consider the catastrophe it had entailed.[2]

Thus it was that throughout the period the constitutional rights of the Estates never stood in the way of the policies of the monarchs: *ratio status* remained the criterion, as much in Oxenstierna's Sweden as in Richelieu's France. A main reason for this state of affairs was undoubtedly the personalities of the monarchs who ruled Sweden between 1600 and 1718. Of all the assets which made the Age of Greatness possible, this was certainly not the least. They were, no doubt, a richly varied collection: it would be difficult to imagine personalities more unlike than those of Charles IX, Christina and Charles XI. But beneath the surface differences they all had certain qualities in common, and those qualities counted for much in the history of the age. They had, one and all, a supreme confidence in their ability to rule: Charles XI might be conscious of the deficiencies of his education, but it did not inhibit him from directing affairs. With the exception of Christina, they all displayed a high level of administrative ability. Every one of them was a soldier by temperament – even Christina, who, doubling the parts of Minerva and Bellona, on one occasion put herself forward as a candidate for the Polish throne with the promise that she would herself lead the armies of the Republic into battle. Charles IX, no doubt, was a bad general, who characteristically blamed the disaster of Kirkholm upon his subordinates; but he had progressive views on tactics and armaments. Charles XI saved his country at Lund more by personal valour and example than by any tactical ability. But Gustav Adolf, Charles X and Charles XII were among the great commanders of the age. And all of them, whatever their military gifts, possessed abnormal (and sometimes terrifying) strength of charac-

[1] *Prästeståndets riksdagsprotokoll*, III.223, for a forceful exposition of this view by Bishop Terserus, 15 September 1675.

[2] Ulf Sjödell, *Kungamakt och högaristokrati. En studie i Sveriges inre historia under Karl XI* (Lund 1966), pp. 9, 13–15, 138, 219–22, 330–2; G. Jonasson, *Karl XII och hans rådgivare* (Uppsala 1960), pp. 261–3.

ter. The volcanic Vasa temperament was present in them all, ready to burst out in formidable eruption upon some incalculable and often trivial occasion: only Charles X and Charles XII really schooled themselves to control it. And as their armies triumphed in the field, so at home they beat down all opposition. Gustav Adolf captured Axel Oxenstierna as a planet captures some asteroid whose orbit has too nearly approached its own, and by doing so for a time emasculated the historic tradition of aristocratic constitutionalism. Charles X and Charles XI imposed the *reduktion* upon the high nobility. Most remarkable of all was the achievement of Christina, who forced through the choice of Charles X as successor in the face of the compact resistance of the chancellor, the Council, the aristocracy, and the initial reluctance of the Estates. Over and over again these monarchs imposed their will on the country: neither the objections of the nobility, nor the sufferings of the masses, deflected them for a moment from their purposes. The most powerful elements in society were confronted and outfaced. Charles XI smashed the high aristocracy by a sustained act of will, as once Gustav Vasa had smashed the church. Charles XII silenced the clamour of a whole nation by a curt message of disapproval despatched from the other end of Europe. Any lingering notion that the king might be no more that *primus inter pares* had no chance against these terrible rulers. No king after Gustav Adolf consented to grant an Accession Charter after the model of 1611: Charles XII did not grant one at all. No adult sovereign ever consented to be bound by the Form of Government of 1634. After two long minorities the authority of the crown remained absolutely undimmed; and Christina, if it had suited her purposes, could have sloughed off Axel Oxenstierna as easily as Charles XI was to dispense with Magnus Gabriel de la Gardie: the greatest statesman of the age was snubbed and silenced by a girl of twenty. Charles XII could be absent from his kingdom for fifteen years, and return to find his authority as absolute as ever. One body in the state, and one only, could claim to have defeated the crown; and that was the church. The church had wrecked John III's religious policy; it had helped to drive Sigismund from his kingdom; it had fought Charles IX to a stalemate; it had blocked Gustav Adolf's plan for a *consistorium generale*; its unyielding attitude helped to make Christina's abdication inevitable. Yet even here the monarchy had the last word; and not the least of the achievements of the absolutism of Charles XI was to reduce the church to the crown's obedient and devoted collaborator.

The strength of the monarchy rested in the last resort upon the fact that it was popular, *völkisch*. These kings were all accessible to their people; some of them had a strong strain of demagogic oratory: almost all could easily make contact with the common man (or, in the case of Charles X, woman); but at the same time they all had a high notion of their royal dignity, and all, by sheer force of personality rather than by the trappings of royalty, had at their command a majesty which was effortless and innate.

Not long ago I came across a casual sentence in a book by a contemporary Swedish author[1] – and one, moreover, who as a writer of historical novels might have been expected to know better – in which mention was made of 'the sorry procession of Swedish kings'. The author is a republican, and perhaps has criteria of his own. But it is difficult to point to any country in seventeenth-century Europe which can show a succession of rulers which can be compared to the Swedish monarchy for sheer capacity for ruling and the determination to rule. Of every one of them it can be said that his personal character and predilections set a stamp upon his reign, and directly affected the fortunes of his subjects. If an imperial history demands leadership for its fulfilment, the Swedish monarchy provided it in abundant measure.

[1] Lars Widding, *På Årstafruns tid* (pocket edn 1973), p. 139.

III

The Character of the Empire

BY 1660, then, the empire had attained its limits and assumed its
final form. In comparison with those empires which were
simultaneously taking shape in the East Indies and beyond the
Atlantic, it was no doubt of modest dimensions: metropolitan
Sweden (to say nothing of Finland) covered a much greater area
than the provinces which had now been added to it. But it was,
nevertheless, quite big enough: too big, indeed, for ease of
integrated government. To the citizen of Stade or Dorpat,
Stockholm must have seemed reassuringly remote; and for the
purposes of administration – as likewise for the direction of
continental war – it was certainly inconveniently peripheral:
already in the 1630s Salvius was suggesting transferring the
direction of foreign affairs to Hamburg, since that city was at once
the centre of financial operations, a nodal point in the European
postal system, and a base for Swedish political and commercial
espionage;[1] and at about the same time Axel Oxenstierna toyed
with the notion of establishing a second capital – a kind of
Swedish Byzantium – at Narva.[2] Nothing came of these ideas;
but they serve to remind us of the physical difficulties in the way
of a measure of control of this aggregate of heterogeneous
territories. The Swedish empire does not fit easily into any
political category: its closest analogue, perhaps, is the empire of
the Habsburgs.[3] There was the same Babel of tongues – Finnish,
Russian, Estonian, Lettish, German, Danish; and if there was one
language which could be called a *lingua franca*, that language was
German rather than Swedish: even in Narva, which was more
Swedish in character than any other town in the empire, Swedish

---

[1] S. Tunberg et al., *Den svenska utrikesförvaltningens historia* (Uppsala 1935), p. 58.

[2] RRP VIII.126; X.56.

[3] I am indebted to Professor Steve Koblik for an even better suggestion; the empire
of the Tsars.

83

did not become the official language of the municipality until as
late as 1684, and in 1690 it was laid down that not *more* than half
the town council should be German.[1] There were the same
violent contrasts between one province and another, in wealth,
level of civilization and local customs. On the one hand Ingria,
barren, empty and barbarous; on the other, Bremen–Verden,
urbanized, with developed institutions and long traditions of
civility; or Skåne, with its rich cornfields, its Renaissance castles,
and an aristocracy polished by proximity to its old metropolis in
Copenhagen. Nevertheless, the territorial acquisitions fell naturally into three groups, each with its own character. First there were
the provinces conquered from Denmark: societies broadly similar
to the imperial power, likely sooner or later to be integrated into
metropolitan Sweden in much the same degree as Wales became
integrated in the sixteenth century. Next, the Baltic provinces –
Kexholm, Ingria, Estonia, Livonia – for whom Swedish rule
provided the first sovereign authority to be common to them
all: here, for the most part, an alien landlord class of German origin
exploited peasant populations of different speech and primitive
culture, while the old Hanseatic towns of the coastlands fought
to preserve their privileges and their commercial traditions against
their new masters. Lastly there were the German lands – Western
Pomerania, Wismar, Bremen–Verden – possession of which
made the crown of Sweden a member of no less than three Circles
of the Empire. The three groups differed fundamentally in
political traditions, interests and way of life: Bremen–Verden was
as little concerned for the fate of Livonia as Cleves for the fate
of East Prussia; Estonia was unmoved by the political passions of
Germany. Three things, all the same, linked the German and the
Baltic lands together. One was the fact that their principal towns,
from Stade to Reval, had in the past been members of the Hanse,
and had in varying measure inherited Hanseatic commercial
attitudes. Another was the institution of serfdom, which stretched,
in differing degrees of severity, almost unbroken from the Neva
to the Elbe. And the third was the Lutheran religion, which
(except for Ingria) was common to them all.

It was something, no doubt, that they should have even so
much in common; but it was scarcely a strong enough cement

---

[1] Arnold Soom, 'Die merkantilistische Wirtschaftspolitik Schwedens und die
baltischen Städte im 17. Jahrhundert', *Jahrbücher für Geschichte Osteuropas* 1963, p. 190.

to hold an empire together. Two of these common features, at all events, were calculated rather to alienate them from the Swedish authorities than to serve as a bond between them. For that right of emporium which was so prized by the Baltic towns certainly did not square with Sweden's commercial aspirations; and the institution of serfdom was repugnant to Swedish ideas and irreconcilable with her political institutions. But the prospect of implanting a 'Swedish way of life' in these respects (and, indeed, in any) was from the outset unhopeful, since there were never enough Swedes in the provinces to provide a soil from which that way of life might grow. There was, indeed, a thin crust of Swedish administrators and ecclesiastics, who did their best to maintain Swedish as an official language; but the provinces never became in any real sense Swedish colonies. It was not that efforts to that end were wanting, at least in the earlier part of the century. When Ingria passed into Swedish possession in 1617 the country was ravaged and desolate, and the surviving peasants, being of the Greek Orthodox religion, fled in droves over the border to Russia to escape the proselytizing activities of the Swedish Lutheran church.[1] In 1619 Gustav Adolf ordered that all peasants who were known to be *contemplating* flight were to be hanged. Here colonization was urgently necessary if the land were to be of any value to its new masters. The government, which viewed the potential of the Ingrian ports with an optimism which proved to be excessive, sought to induce Russian merchants from Novgorod to come and live in them;[2] and in 1622, by the so-called Capitulation, an attempt was made to attract settlers of all classes.[3] But from this plan of colonization Swedes were specifically excluded: the settlers Gustav Adolf was looking for were Dutch, and above all Germans – men whose 'honest German habits' would serve as a corrective to the 'swinish Russian customs'.[4] Some Germans and Dutchmen did take the bait, but on the whole they did not thrive; and quite early it was found expedient to

---

[1] H. Sepp, 'Bidrag till Ingermanlands historia under 1600-talet', *Svio-Estonica* 1934, p. 78; for the treatment of the Greek Orthodox population, see C. Öhlander, *Om den svenska kyrkoreformationen i Ingermanland* (Uppsala 1912), pp. 12–22.

[2] Arnold Soom, 'De ingermanländska städerna och freden i Stolbova 1617', *Svio-Estonica* 1936, pp. 57–8.

[3] *Ibid.*, 75; Öhlander, *On den svenska kyrkoreformationen*, pp. 2–3.

[4] Styffe, *Konung Gustaf II Adolfs skrifter*, pp. 276–81 (instruction for Nils Assarsson, 6 March 1626).

allow Johan Skytte to import Swedish and Finnish colonists to his great barony of Duderhof.[1] But Ingria remained thinly-populated and poor, and Swedish colonists few. The government did something to remedy the position by making the province a dumping-ground for undesirables: peasants who felled the royal oaks or shot elk, turbulent individuals who refused to pay their taxes or agitated against excessive labour-services, would find themselves transported to Sweden's Botany Bay.[2] But though the provinces may thus have provided pasture for black sheep, they can hardly be said to have constituted the land of opportunity for unsuccessful speculators or the sons of impecunious gentlemen.

The shortage of inhabitants had military as well as fiscal implications, on the long exposed frontier with Russia; and with a view to combining the cultivation of the soil with the organization of defence, military colonies were from time to time established: in Karelia and Ingria first; then on Axel Oxenstierna's estates round Wolmar; and also in Livonia, near Dorpat. Their number increased in the years after 1632, and some were still in existence in 1670; but they can hardly have contributed much to effective colonization.[3] Only in Estonia was there any sizeable migration of Swedes to the new lands: after the peace of Stolbova it had been encouraged by Gustav Adolf's promise of land-grants to those who were prepared to settle.[4] A belt of Swedish colonization established itself along the coastline, and upon the islands of Dagö and Rågö, and already by 1630 it was reckoned that perhaps 17% of the peasants of Estonia were immigrants – Swedish, Finnish or Russian.[5] Most of the Swedes on Dagö were in 1781 transported *en bloc* by Catherine II to the government of

[1] Sepp, *Svio-Estonica* 1934, p. 76; R. Swedlund, *Grev- och friherreskapen i Sverige och Finland* (Uppsala 1936), p. 119; F. C. von Moser, *Neues Patriotisches Archiv für Deutschland*, I (Frankfurt and Leipzig 1786), p. 18.

[2] *RRP* I.22; II.229; XV.7–13; *Vendels sockens dombok*, ed. N. Edling (Uppsala 1925), p. 64; B. Boëthius, *Skogen och bygden* (Stockholm 1939), p. 178.

[3] For the military colonies see *AOSB* II.i.222; II.ix.43; Liljedahl, *Svensk förvaltning i Livland*, p. 57; Wittrock, *Karl XI:s förmyndares finanspolitik*, I, p. 182; Carlson, *Sveriges historia*, II, p. 253 n 1.

[4] B. Federley, *Konung, stathållare och korporationer. Studier i Livlands förvaltning 1581–1600* (Helsinki 1962), p. 52; Hallenberg, *Svea Rikes Historia*, IV, p. 592.

[5] J. Vasar, 'Utvecklingen av böndernas rättsläge i Estland till Karl XI', *Svio-Estonica* 1936, p. 33. In Livonia there were German immigrants too: it was they who rebuilt Dorpat from the ruins and once more provided Kokenhusen with inhabitants; Liljedahl, *Svensk förvaltning i Livland*, pp. 465–6.

Cherson, where at Gammalsvenskby they founded a community which survived to the present century; but the remainder retained their holdings and their identity through many vicissitudes: in 1939 there were still some 8,000 Swedish-speakers on the coast between Baltic Port and Hapsal.[1]

On the whole, then, the Swedish empire lacked those binding and unifying ties of sentiment which link colonies to the motherland: in the German territories, certainly, they were wholly absent. What, then, held the empire together, other than the imposed authority of a foreign power? Had this aggregate of disparate territories any identifiable anatomy of its own? Were there institutions in common? And had the government in Stockholm anything deserving of the name of an imperial policy?

Let us take the last question first. There is no doubt that in the early days, when the empire was confined to the Baltic lands, successive kings of Sweden did have a clearly-formulated imperial design. Estonia had come into Swedish possession by free cession of its inhabitants, and at the time of its acquisition Eric XIV had given explicit confirmation of the privileges of Reval, and of the local nobility. But within the limits of those privileges both he and his immediate successors pursued a double objective: in the first place the full incorporation of the territory into the Swedish realm; and in the second, the modification of Estonian institutions, the transformation of the Estonian way of life, to bring it into line with Swedish practice and traditions – which meant, in fact, the reform of what were felt to be abuses: a programme which from the beginning was difficult to reconcile with that respect for local rights to which they were committed. From the 1580s onwards attempts were made from time to time to persuade or coerce the Estonian nobles and towns to send representatives to the *riksdag*;[2] in 1599 and 1600 resolutions of the *riksdag* were declared to be applicable to Estonia;[3] in 1602 Charles IX insisted upon including a Livonian noble in his reconstituted Council of State.[4] He also pursued a deliberate policy of making large grants

---

[1] Per Söderbäck, *Estlands svenskbygd* (Stockholm 1939), pp. 11–14, 97.

[2] *SRDA* II.964; J. Rosén, 'Statsledning och provinspolitik under Sveriges stormaktstid', *Scandia* 1946, pp. 233–5; N. Ahnlund, 'Die Ostseeprovinzen und der Reichstag Schwedens', in *Pirmā Baltijas Vēsturnieku Konference* (Riga 1938), pp. 420–1.

[3] Ahnlund, 'Die Ostseeprovinzen und der Reichstag Schwedens', pp. 420–1.

[4] Sven A. Nilsson, *På väg mot reduktionen* (Stockholm 1964), p. 43. Subsequently he added six more, giving Livlanders a majority.

of fiefs in Finland to members of the Estonian aristocracy, with
the obvious intention of integrating them into the Swedish–
Finnish nobility: it has been said that in 1608 'there were more
Balt fief-holders in Finland than Finnish and Swedish put
together'.[1] Gustav Adolf in some measure continued his father's
policy: when Riga was captured, in 1621, the town was forced
to pledge itself to send representatives to all meetings of the
riksdag, and for a short time actually did so.[2]

Meanwhile there had already been a long history of attempts
to carry out necessary reforms. Eric XIV in his day had denounced
the abuses of Estonian serfdom, had ordered his bailiffs to harass
(*småhata*) the nobility, and had taken the first steps to curb their
domestic jurisdiction;[3] in 1583 comes the first effort to do
something about the horrifying degradation of the Estonian
church;[4] and soon afterwards John III began to grapple with the
intractable problem of recasting local government on Swedish
models.[5] In 1601 Charles IX, at a *lantdag* in Reval, enunciated a
programme which sums up and amplifies the sporadic initiatives
of his predecessors. It included a parliamentary union; the
introduction of Swedish law; contribution by all classes (including
the nobility) to the building of churches and schools; the throwing
open of educational facilities to the sons of peasants; and, implicit
in all the rest, the abolition of serfdom.[6]

It was an enlightened and courageous assertion of moral values,
civilized standards and Swedish traditions of liberty, flung in the
face of a community which received it with indignant incom-
prehension. They were an entrenched upper class of traders and
landed magnates, German-speaking, alien, lording it over an
enserfed and brutalized population of Ests and Letts. Reval's law

---

[1] *Ibid.*, p. 42; A. Korhonen, 'Om finska rytteriet under Gustaf II Adolf', in *Ny militär
tidskrift*, IV (Stockholm 1931), p. 244.

[2] N. Ahnlund, *Ståndsriksdagens utdaning* (Stockholm 1933), p. 389.

[3] Rosén, 'Statsledning och provinspolitik', pp. 229–30; Alvin Isberg, *Kyrkoförvaltningsproblem i Estland 1561–1700* (Uppsala 1970), p. 20. It was ironical that it was one
of the charges against Eric after his deposition that he wanted to make his Swedish
subjects 'Ests and thralls': *SRDA* II.277–8.

[4] Isberg, *Kyrkoförvaltningsproblem i Estland*, pp. 26, 28.

[5] *Ibid.*, pp. 17–19; Liljedahl, *Svensk förvaltning i Livland*, p. 6; Federley, *Konung,
stathållare och korporationer*, pp. 98–101.

[6] Isberg, *Kyrkoförvaltningsproblem i Estland*, pp. 51–2; Liljedahl, *Svensk förvaltning i
Livland*, pp. 11–12.

was the law of Lübeck, and not until 1614 was it finally established that the ultimate appeal lay not to Lübeck but to Stockholm;[1] in the countryside the nobility regulated their affairs according to the so-called 'Harrien-Wierland' code. The presentation to livings was in the hands of town-councils or landlords, who often chose scandalous clergy ignorant of the language of their flocks. The churches could neither be rebuilt nor maintained, because the lords refused to allow their peasantry to pay tithe lest they might default on their dues to their masters; and they themselves would make no contribution whatever: small wonder if paganism was not unusual. In their condition of bondage to their German lords the peasants attached a special significance to the old heathen festivals: when they buried one of themselves they placed food in the grave, with the words: 'Fare hence, poor soul, from this condition to a better world, where the Germans no longer shall rule over thee, but thou shalt rule over them. Here hast thou a sword, food and journey-money' – a practice which is said to have continued until far into the seventeenth century.[2] Towns and nobles formed 'corporations', strongly organized, stubbornly determined to maintain their privileges; and for the moment they prevailed. In the face of their compact resistance Charles IX, deeply involved in a disastrous war with Poland, dependent upon the cooperation of the Estonian nobility for military aid, was in no position to put his programme into effect.

It was an easier matter in Ingria after 1617. Here there was no strong local nobility, no inconvenient privileges, a territory ravaged, depopulated, prostrate. Here was a *tabula rasa*, and the government could write what it would. Swedish law, Swedish administrative patterns, were simply imposed: in Narva they had been imposed long before.[3] But the devastated condition of the province made it imperative to ensure an adequate supply of labour: the peasant therefore remained bound to the soil, though serfdom never established itself, and the strong hand of Swedish justice might be supposed to mitigate some of the worst evils. At

[1] Isberg, *Kyrkoförvaltningsproblem i Estland*, p. 53.

[2] J. Blees, *Gustaf II Adolf och Estland* (Norrköping 1932), p. 35.

[3] A. C. Meurling, *Svensk domstolsförvaltning i Livland 1623–1700* (Lund 1967), pp. 76–7; Rosén, 'Statsledning och provinspolitik', p. 249; Öhlander, *Om den svenska kyrkoreformationen*, pp. 9–12.

first it seemed that the same methods might be applied in Livonia
too. Livonia, like Ingria, was a conquered province; it had suffered
terribly from the great famine at the beginning of the century,
as well as from the incessant wars: it is estimated that at the time
of the Swedish conquest three-quarters of the peasant farms were
vacant and desolate.[1] The land had not been ceded upon terms;
except in regard to Riga local privileges could be brushed aside;
the local organs of the nobility – the *lantdag* and *lantråd* – which
were so strong in Estonia, had here for a time ceased to function
effectively, and the type of aristocratic self-government that
existed in Estonia could be – and for a time was – prohibited.
Social and ecclesiastical conditions were fully as bad as in Estonia;
and Skytte was to describe the clergy as 'so monstrous that they
beggar description'.[2] The need for reform was obvious; the
moment seemed propitious.

In 1627 began a full-scale effort to set right what was amiss.
Johannes Rudbeckius, the formidable bishop of Västerås, was sent
to Estonia to reform the church in that province;[3] simultaneously
a commission was sent over to deal with non-ecclesiastical abuses
both in Estonia and Livonia; and three years later Johan Skytte
began his memorable tenure of office as Livonia's Governor-
General. These initiatives represented a revival of the ideals and
policies of Charles IX, whose tradition Skytte in more than one
respect embodied; and Skytte summed up the programme with
which he set out in the phrase '*unus rex, una lex, et grex unus*'.[4]
The task was daunting; the success, alas, only partial. The
overpowering personality and abrasive zeal of Rudbeckius aroused
the bitter hostility of the corporations;[5] the commission's experiences in Estonia were so discouraging that they came home
without tackling Livonia at all. But Skytte stayed; and in spite
of everything went far towards realizing the programme with
which he had set out.[6] Swedish law became (officially, at any rate)

[1] Vasar, 'Utvecklingen av böndernas rättsläge', p. 27.   [2] *AOSB* II.x.341.
[3] Blees, *Gustav II Adolf och Estland*, pp. 55–87; F. Westling, 'Estlands kyrka
1571–1644', *Kyrkohistorisk årsskrift* XXI (Uppsala 1921), pp. 190–5; Isberg, *Kyrkoförvaltningsproblem i Estland*, pp. 55–83; Liljedahl, *Svensk förvaltning i Livland*, pp. 193ff.
[4] Liljedahl, *Svensk förvaltning i Livland*, p. 532.
[5] When he returned to Sweden he was obliged to confess 'Curavimus Babylonae,
et non sanata est': Westling, 'Estlands kyrka 1571–1644', pp. 2–3.
[6] Liljedahl, *Svensk förvaltning i Livland*, pp. 269, 289–91, 324, 365, 387–9, 394, 534;
Meurling, *Svensk domstolsförvaltning i Livland*, pp. 17–19, 43–8, 80–3; B. Swartling,
Georg Stiernhielm, hans lif och verksamhet (Uppsala 1909), p. 27.

the norm, and a new Supreme Court for Livonia and Ingria was established at Dorpat to administer it. Local government was reorganized on lines approximating to the Swedish model, though attempts to induce the major towns to accept 'royal' burgomasters and municipal *collegia*, after the Swedish pattern, were rebuffed in Reval and Riga, and were successful only in Narva.[1] Gustav Adolf's Magdeburg Church Ordinance was henceforth to regulate ecclesiastical affairs, and a mixed *consistorium generale*, of the type which he had tried but failed to establish in Sweden, was instituted to apply it. *Gymnasia* were established in Riga and Reval; and in 1632 there was founded the University of Dorpat – the last, and not the least remarkable, of Gustav Adolf's services to education. Here for the first time a real effort was made to cater for the educational needs of the oppressed native populations: courses in Estonian and Lettish were provided; and despite the bitter opposition of the nobility, the University was from the beginning thrown open to the sons of peasants.[2] The whole achievement was a record of which any colonial governor might have been proud. But the main evils persisted. Without adequate financial resources the work of social and educational reform could not be carried through; and the nobility would neither contribute to that reform nor allow their peasantry to do so. And serfdom remained – softened, no doubt, by the regulation of traditional relationships upon a basis of certain law, as against the arbitrary tyranny of the lords, and limited by Gustav Adolf's stern prohibition of any attempt to extend it to the Swedish colonists.[3] But as the political situation had thwarted the efforts of Charles IX, so it aborted the reforms of Skytte: Gustav Adolf, like his father, could not risk the total alienation of the Baltic nobility, and more than once Skytte received sharp warnings to temper his reforming zeal.[4]

Thus the state of affairs in Livonia bore some resemblance to that which is familiar from the history of other empires: the metropolitan power attempts, against strong provincial opposi-

---

[1] Soom, 'Die merkantilistische Wirtschaftspolitik Schwedens', pp. 187–9.

[2] J. Bergman, *Universitet i Dorpat under den svenska tiden* (Uppsala 1932); Liljedahl, *Svensk förvaltning i Livland*, pp. 398–406.   [3] *Ibid.*, p. 228.

[4] Vasar, 'Utvecklingen av böndernas rättsläge', pp. 31–2; Liljedahl, *Svensk förvaltning i Livland*, pp. 310, 528: he warned Skytte to 'apply himself to gaining a good understanding of *naturam gentis* and *genius loci* before enacting or altering anything of consequence'.

tion, to apply standards of civilized behaviour which to the provincials seem inappropriate, and indeed impracticable in the local context. Up to a point, the attempt is successful; but sooner or later the stage is reached at which reform conflicts with political expediency, and in the clash of interests it is expediency that prevails. The Baltic nobility, in addition to their racial exclusiveness, class pride and fierce tenacity of privilege, had something of the frontiersman mentality in their dislike of governance and their impatience of obligations, fiscal or moral. They looked upon their Estonian peasantry as the Boers looked on the Hottentots; Rudbeckius was their Dr John Philip; Skytte was their Maynier. Baltic nationalist historians have been almost as grudging in their appreciation of the reforming efforts of the imperial power as the new school of British imperial historians of the efforts of the missionaries; and both, perhaps, stand in need of correction.

This becomes clear from a consideration of imperial policy in the half-century which followed Skytte's return to Sweden in 1634. It would be unfair to call it a policy of abdication of responsibility; but certainly it could entail that consequence. Undoubtedly it represents a sharp reversal of the approach to the imperial problem which had been personified in Charles IX and Johan Skytte. That reversal was inaugurated by the Form of Government of 1634. For although the Form of Government included clauses which placed the *landshövdingar* in all the Baltic provinces on the same footing as those in Sweden, and laid upon them (except in the case of Estonia) the same obligations,[1] in one essential particular it marked a sharp swing away from the objectives of the previous half-century, in that clause 46 laid it down that no person not ordinarily resident in Sweden or Finland might henceforward be a member of the *riksdag* or the Council. Integration now seemed finally barred. With the death of Gustav Adolf, and the return of Skytte to Sweden, another political tradition had come into its own: high-aristocratic, exclusive, decentralizing; the tradition of the adversaries whom Charles IX had brought to the block at Linköping in 1600. Of that tradition Axel Oxenstierna – Skytte's personal and political enemy – was

[1] Clauses 23, 37. The Instruction for Local Government of 1635 was also intended to apply in Livonia, but only in so far as it did not conflict with local custom and usage: Meurling, *Svensk domstolsförvaltning i Livland*, pp. 17–19.

(in this instance) the mouthpiece. Under the influence of these views the attack on the provincial corporations slackened; realism won an apparently final victory over idealism; and the movement for reform, though not wholly abandoned, was pursued with elaborate caution and diminished vigour. Neither incorporation nor uniformity would for half a century be regarded as desirable objectives.

By the mid-thirties the Livonian nobility was beginning to recover from the disintegrating experiences of the twenties; and in 1643 it was permitted to hold the first *lantdag* since the Swedish conquest. Ironically enough it used its partially-recovered self-government to demand the incorporation which it had hitherto resisted. The reception of this proposal by Axel Oxenstierna was verbally ambiguous,[1] but in effect a decisive rejection. Neither he nor his high-aristocratic allies relished the prospect of a flood of Balts into the *Riddarhus*. Nor had they any wish for uniformity in the matter of privileges, if that meant a reduction of Livonian privilege to the Swedish level. And this for a very cogent reason. They were themselves, very many of them, Livonian landholders, and on the largest scale; they were the beneficiaries of the crown's lavish donations of conquered territory. Axel Oxenstierna's estates in Livonia amounted to about one-eighth of the whole area of the province. They felt an agreeable and unfamiliar ease in the loose garments of Livonian privileges. Oxenstierna had his own domainial courts (though no such jurisdiction had ever been granted him), and sharply rebuffed any attempt by the king's justices to interfere.[2] Many of his colleagues shared his feelings: it was significant that his brother, and also Per Banér, had condemned Rudbeckius' intemperate attacks on the Baltic nobility.[3] It was significant also that Oxenstierna himself had disapproved of the liberal principles upon which Skytte and Gustav Adolf had founded the University of Dorpat.[4]

---

[1] *RRP* x.182; *cf. ibid.* viii.180. So ambiguous, that Odhner believed that he was in favour of it: Odhner, *Sveriges inre historia*, p. 346. But see Rosén, 'Statsledning och provinspolitik', p. 245.

[2] Meurling, *Svensk domstolsförvaltning i Livland*, p. 78; and *cf. AOSB* i.v.323. His grant of Wenden is in *AOSB* ii.i.750. For donations in Livonia, see Liljedahl, *Svensk förvaltning i Livland*, pp. 43–5.

[3] Liljedahl, *Svensk förvaltning i Livland*, p. 225.

[4] N. Runeby, *Monarchia mixta* (Uppsala 1962), pp. 269, 389.

So the Livonian request for integration was turned down; and when it was renewed in 1662 it was turned down again. For more than three decades the government trod very warily in the Baltic provinces – as, for instance, in 1661, when they beat a hasty retreat in the face of opposition to a projected Stamp Act.[1] Oxenstierna's caution effectively hampered the attempts of Bishop Jheringius to carry a measure of church reform in Estonia;[2] Erik Oxenstierna was sent to Reval as Governor-General in 1646 well primed with paternal advice against running his head upon brick walls.[3] In this climate of opinion uniformity made little progress in Livonia, and in Estonia came to a dead stop: the litigious inhabitants of that province luxuriated in at least three different systems of law; the land was in the hands of the nobility; the towns abated nothing of their privileges; education and church reform lagged miserably; and – except for the Swedish colonists – the rural population continued in serfdom.

But if under these auspices uniformity and incorporation made no progress in the Baltic lands, under no conceivable auspices were they attainable in the German territories acquired in 1648. The terms of the peace of Westphalia straitly circumscribed Sweden's room for manoeuvre in this matter.[4] Both Bremen–Verden and Pomerania remained members of the *Reich*, with all the obligations attendant upon membership – indeed, it was precisely the Emperor's anxiety that those obligations should be discharged, at a moment when Austria was threatened by a Turkish invasion, that induced him in 1664 to grant the long-delayed investiture to the Swedish crown.[5] Each had its local privileges guaranteed in the terms of the peace settlement. Their law was the law and custom of the Holy Roman Empire: there could be no question here of the introduction of Swedish law or Swedish legal forms,

---

[1] Meurling, *Svensk domstolsförvaltning i Livland*, pp. 160–8.

[2] Isberg, *Kyrkoförvaltningsproblem i Estland*, pp. 95ff, 108–20.

[3] Ellen Fries, *Erik Oxenstierna* (Stockholm 1889), pp. 77–8.

[4] For Pomerania and Bremen–Verden, see in general Pär-Erik Back, *Herzog und Landschaft. Politische Ideen und Verfassungsprogramme in Schwedisch-Pommern um die Mitte des 17. Jahrhunderts* (Lund 1955); id., 'Striden om nebenmodus. En studie i Karl XI:s pommerske finanspolitik', *KFÅ* 1958; K.-R. Böhme, *Bremisch–Verdische Staatsfinanzen 1645–76* (Uppsala 1967); H. Backhaus, *Reichsterritorium und schwedische Provinz. Vorpommern unter Karl XI:s Vormündern* (Göttingen 1969); Edvard A. Zetterqvist, *Grundläggningen af det svenska väldet i hertigdömena Bremen och Verden* (Oskarshamn 1891).

[5] Backhaus, *Reichsterritorium und schwedische Provinz*, p. 137.

no appeal to *Svea Hovrätt*. It is true that appeal to the *Reichs-kammergericht* was no longer available to them, for by the terms of the peace the Swedish crown had secured the *privilegium de non appellando*; but this had been accorded only on the understanding that a court of appeal for both territories should be set up in Germany. Hence the creation of a Supreme Court at Wismar in 1653, with a budget defrayed equally by Pomerania and by Bremen–Verden.[1] One trivial example may serve to demonstrate the reality of the continuing relationship of Sweden's German territories with the *Reich*. When in the early fifties the authorities in Pomerania were trying to set some limits to the ragging of freshmen at the University of Greifswald, they could do so only by application to the Emperor through the Swedish ambassador at Regensburg. The application was successful, and an imperial edict of 1654 abolished (or purported to abolish) ragging at all the universities of Germany.[2]

Pomerania was a former ally, which had come to Sweden by treaty and was officially termed an 'acquired' province; Bremen–Verden had been conquered; but there was here no difference corresponding to that produced by the analogous distinction between Estonia and Livonia. They were both very typical German states of the middling order, each with its Estates, each with *Landräthe* to act as the executive committee of the Nobility and the advisory organ of government; each with constitutional traditions, stronger in Pomerania, weaker in Bremen–Verden. The Swedish monarchs ruled in them as dukes, and they inherited the political attitudes and constitutional quarrels of their pre-decessors – quarrels which were no concern of the king of Sweden, and still less of the Swedish *riksdag*. In both provinces the constitutional situation was viewed in dualistic terms, with the respective rights of duke and Estates grounded upon past history, though with some still-debatable ground between. There was the typical separation of military finance (under the control of the duke) from civil finance (under the control of the Estates) which is familiar from the history of Brandenburg; and the new Swedish

---

[1] The establishment of a *Generaldirektorium* for both provinces, also to be located at Wismar, was also contemplated in 1651, but the idea was not pursued: Zetterqvist, *Grundläggningen af det svenska väldet*, p. 174.

[2] Ivar Seth, *Universitetet i Greifswald och dess ställning i svensk kulturpolitik 1637–1815* (Uppsala 1952), p. 56.

rulers never seriously tried to change it. A main concern of the Estates was the assertion of the right of inhabitants of the duchies to a monopoly of office (*Indigenatsrecht*), and by extension their right to nominate to appointments; but the former, at least, was readily conceded.[1] No attempt was made to Swedify the civil service; German in effect remained the official language, except in the Pomeranian Treasury, which was staffed by Stockholm-trained experts, and conducted its business in Swedish.[2] The duchies managed their affairs without much reference to the royal government in Stockholm; legislation and taxation was by the local Estates; and if ordinances were to be issued, they emanated from the duke, not from the king of Sweden. Both duchies strove to secure acknowledgement of their right to opt out of inconvenient involvements in Swedish foreign policy; both professed that what happened in other provinces of the empire was no concern of theirs; both aspired to the same kind of position as that enjoyed by Hanover *vis-à-vis* Great Britain after 1714, except that neither maintained diplomatic representatives in Stockholm, as Hanover did in London. But on foreign policy, at least, the dukes could make no concessions, for (as we shall see in the next chapter) the duchies were deemed to be of capital importance for the maintenance of Sweden's position as a great power.

Otherwise, the relations of the dukes with their new German subjects were surprisingly and consistently good. They appear to have felt no resentment at subjection to a foreign ruler; for indeed he ruled in the style of other princes of Germany, and was scarcely felt to be a foreigner at all. When they bickered with him on constitutional issues, the disputes ran on reassuringly familiar and characteristically German lines. The dukes were no doubt in a stronger position than their ineffective predecessors, for in both duchies they were able to keep sizeable standing armies on foot; but also in a weaker, in that massive alienations of ducal estates and revenues left them financially more at the Estates' mercy:[3]

---

[1] Pomerania enjoyed a kind of reciprocal *Indigenatsrecht* with Sweden, which (at least in theory) meant that Pomeranians could obtain posts in Sweden, and even (despite the Form of Government!) enter the *Riddarhus*: Backhaus, *Reichsterritorium und schwedische Provinz*, p. 143.   [2] *Ibid.*, pp. 85–6.

[3] In Bremen–Verden Christina's donations (mostly of church lands) went to 36 soldiers, 29 civil servants in Stockholm or Stade, 3 princes, 6 foreign diplomats, 6

this was especially the case in Pomerania, where the extensive allocation of *Tafelgüter* to Queen Christina on her abdication made a balanced budget almost impossible until they fell in to the crown at her death in 1689.[1]

In 1652 Bremen–Verden was given a compact, economical and efficient administration, modelled on the Swedish collegial system; but neither here nor in Pomerania was any serious attempt made to modify the established constitutional dualism. Under stress of war Charles X undoubtedly behaved on occasion in a high-handed manner which his German subjects felt to be despotic; but this proved to be an uncharacteristic episode. The normal pattern was rather one of compromise and reciprocal concessions: indeed, it was an established constitutional convention in Pomerania that if the duke and the Estates failed to reach agreement, the matter fell away. This was the spirit which informed the settlements of 1663, when both duchies were given constitutions whereby the duke promised to rule only through the Estates, and to levy no taxes for civil purposes without their consent; settlements which proved so durable that they long survived Sweden's existence as a great power.[2] The Regents for Charles XI were remarkably careful to respect Pomerania's privileges: in so far as they were ignored or overridden they were so because Karl-Gustaf Wrangel, who governed the duchy for the whole of the period, was a tough soldier who was not prepared to allow constitutional niceties to stand in the way of military necessities, and was quite prepared to disobey and defy the government in Stockholm if he thought proper.[3] Before 1680 the government took care not to antagonize the Pomeranian nobility by interfering with the exploitation of their peasantry: possibly, it has been suggested, because it would have been embarrassing

---

doctors of medicine, 6 nobles, 2 Danish officials, 7 students, the town of Stade, one man of learning, one master-cook, and five others: more than half of these recipients were German: Zetterqvist, *Grundläggningen af det svenska väldet*, pp. 105–6.

[1] G. H. von Essen, *Alienationer och reduktioner i f.d. svenska Pommern* (Stockholm 1900), pp. 34, 59–61, 64, 67.

[2] In return, the Estates abandoned their opposition to the duke's keeping a standing army, and agreed that the much-disliked excise be continued. In 1669 Pomerania accepted a fixed budget for the ensuing five years: Wittrock, *Karl XI:s förmyndares finanspolitik*, II, p. 231.

[3] Backhaus, *Reichsterritorium und schwedische Provinz*, pp. 81, 212–22.

for Sweden if they had retorted by appealing to the Emperor.[1]
And though Charles XI once irritably complained of the Pomeranians' eternal insistence on their statutes and privileges, 'as
though they were not our subjects but a separate republic, with
which we are obliged formally to negotiate',[2] relations remained
reasonably harmonious, even under the strain of the *reduktion*.
Charles XI's absolutism made trade easier for the Pomeranian
towns, and extended its favour to the ruling burgher oligarchies
– no doubt because some of the leading citizens were its creditors.[3]
The difference between the constitutional situation in Pomerania
and that in the Baltic provinces was well illustrated in 1699, when
Sweden was preparing for a possible war with Denmark over
Holstein–Gottorp. It was then decided that the cost of maintaining
the troops sent over from Sweden to Pomerania should be borne,
not by the Pomeranian, but by the Swedish Treasury. But when
it was proposed at the same time to send some regiments from
Finland to Estonia, it was taken for granted that they must be
supported by the province.[4]

In Germany, then, there could be no question of pursuing such
a policy of uniformity as had been designed for the Baltic lands.
Nevertheless, when it came to the basic anatomy of empire there
was not a great deal of difference between the two regions; and
this for the reason that in both that anatomy was of a relatively
rudimentary kind. There was no council or College in Stockholm
whose special business it was to take care of imperial affairs in
general, though the Chancery maintained a special section for the
Baltic lands, and another for Pomerania partly staffed by
Pomeranians.[5] The Council of State decided cases which came to
it on petition to the king for revision of judgments in the
provincial courts. The Treasury drew up detailed budgets for the

---

[1] Jan Peters, 'Unter der schwedischen Krone. Zum 150. Jahrstag der Beendigung
der Schwedenherrschaft in Pommern', *Zeitschrift für Geschichtswissenschaft* XIV (1966),
p. 36.

[2] Oscar Malmström, *Nils Bielke såsom Generalguvernör i Pommern 1687–1697* (Stockholm and Lund 1896), p. 45.

[3] Peters, 'Unter der schwedischen Krone', p. 39.

[4] James Cavallie, *Från fred till krig. De finansiella problemen kring krigsutbrottet år 1700*
(Uppsala 1975), pp. 84, 179.

[5] Seth, *Universitetet i Greifswald*, p. 15; Arne Munthe in *Kungl. Maj:ts Kanslis historia*,
I (Uppsala 1935), 104.

provinces, and left it to the provincial authorities to negotiate with the local Estates for raising the money; it checked contracts and crown rents; it handled customs revenues; and it insisted on an annual audit in Stockholm. From the beginning it had been a principle of government that each province should be financially self-supporting;[1] and after 1660 there were reiterated demands, at *riksdag* after *riksdag*, that they should really be so.[2] It was an inequitable requirement, since all the provinces had suffered from involvement in Sweden's wars, and since one main argument for their acquisition was precisely that they acted as buffer-zones to protect the Swedish taxpayer from the cost of self-defence. Indeed, it proved not merely inequitable but unrealistic, at least for the greater part of the period. Taken as a whole, the provinces of the empire usually were in fact more or less self-supporting; but they differed too much in wealth, living-standards, and the scale of government expenditure to be individually amenable to such a rule.[3] There was a perennial deficit in Ingria, mainly because all crown lands in that province had been alienated to the nobility;[4] and Wismar was never in a condition to balance its budget. Until 1689 this was also the case with Pomerania, partly because of the alienation of the *Tafelgüter* to Queen Christina, but also because expenditure in Germany on troops and fortifications was exceptionally heavy: in 1662, for instance, the budgets for the German provinces totalled 524,330 *d.s.m.*; those for the Baltic provinces, 407,530; as against 1,996,880 for Sweden and Finland. And whereas less than half of the Swedish budget went on military expenses, in the provinces they exceeded the civil expenses in the ratio of more than 4 to 1:[5] in Pomerania they accounted for more than three-quarters of the total.[6] In these circumstances a measure of intra-imperial financial integration became necessary: Estonia and Livonia contributed largely to cover the deficits in Ingria, Wismar and Pomerania (in 1686 as

---

[1] The principle was formulated for Estonia as early as 1626: Liljedahl, *Svensk förvaltning i Livland*, p. 182. Financial control from Stockholm can be seen as early as 1587: Federley, *Konung, stathållare och korporationer*, p. 21.

[2] E.g. *SRARP* IX.97; XII.267.

[3] Wittrock, *Karl XI:s förmyndares finanspolitik*, II, pp. 284–5.

[4] *Ibid.*, II, p. 80; Cavallie, *Från fred till krig*, p. 25.

[5] Wittrock, *Karl XI:s förmyndares finanspolitik*, I, p. 149.

[6] Backhaus, *Reichsterritorium und schwedische Provinz*, p. 198.

much as 200,000 *d.s.m.*);[1] in 1697–9 Bremen subsidized the Treasury at Wismar to the tune of 131,000 *d.s.m.*;[2] and in 1669 the Swedish Treasury made itself responsible for 90% of Pomerania's military expenditure.[3] It was, no doubt, a somewhat hand-to-mouth system. But it was flexible; on the whole it worked; and in the existing circumstances it was perhaps as satisfactory an expedient as could be devised. Apart from this financial management, the provinces were subject to control from Stockholm only in the matter of appointments to a handful of senior posts in their administrations, the direction of military and naval arrangements, and the strategy of commerce.

Commerce, it is true, was a conceivable unifying force: though the formal political articulation might be slender, it was possible to envisage the reality of a trading empire. Axel Oxenstierna certainly saw the empire in such terms.[4] The College of Commerce, which was established in 1651, was designed by him to be a body which should unify and direct the whole trade and industry of the empire. In its original shape the plan clearly contemplated a procedure of intra-imperial consultation on commercial matters; for in addition to the College in Stockholm there were to be two other miniature Colleges, one for the Baltic lands, and one for the German. The three were to work in close collaboration, and the two provincial Colleges were to send an assessor to Stockholm once a year, for report and consultation. This part of the plan was never pursued; but it is symptomatic of the imperial idea which lay behind it that the Stockholm College was in fact partly financed by the tolls taken at Reval.[5] The Stockholm College did indeed do some of the things which it had been designed to do: after 1667, for instance, it dealt with all cases of maritime law; it attempted (though without much success) to impose on the Baltic provinces the strict specialization

---

[1] Wittrock, *Karl XI:s förmyndares finanspolitik*, I, p. 212; Carlson, *Sveriges historia*, IV, p. 285.

[2] Cavallie, *Från fred till krig*, p. 24; and *cf.* Wittrock, *Karl XI:s förmyndares finanspolitik*, I, p. 288.

[3] Backhaus, *Reichsterritorium und schwedische Provinz*, p. 297.

[4] For Oxenstierna's Instruction see Stiernman, *Samling utaf Bref...angående... Commerce*, II, pp. 669–76.

[5] Joh. Ax. Almquist, *Kommerskollegium och Riksens ständers Manufakturkontor 1651–1910*, I (Stockholm 1912), pp. 17, 21, 51, 54.

of trades and professions which was the rule in Sweden;[1] by granting short-term monopolies it encouraged the setting up of industrial undertakings around Narva and Riga;[2] it revised and simplified duties; and in 1697 it optimistically promulgated a schedule of tolls for the whole empire.[3]

But behind Axel Oxenstierna's Instruction lay much more than a desire for the rationalization of administration and the unification of policy. In the Introduction to that Instruction he had unrolled a magnificent perspective of commercial development springing from the uniquely advantageous geographical position of the Swedish realm. After 1648 Sweden controlled every major port on the Baltic except Königsberg and Danzig; she held in her grip the estuary of every major river from the Neva to the Weser, with the single exception of the Vistula. This situation, he believed, must have as its consequence that all the products of a vast upland would naturally drain towards the ports of the empire: from Muscovy, the Ukraine, Lithuania, Silesia, Bohemia, Germany – perhaps even from Italy – the trade-routes led inevitably to Swedish ports, and the traders of western Europe who came to purchase the exports of these regions must pay the Swedish customs-dues in order to secure them. The empire, as he saw it, could be welded into a single economic system. Not that it was any part of Swedish policy to set up a coercive monopoly of these trades: on the contrary, Oxenstierna believed that trade should be left to find its own way without attempts by politicians to control it.[4] It should rather be the aim of governments to encourage traders of all nations, and to remove obstacles to commerce wherever possible – as Sweden had done, for instance, at Narva, and at the new foundation of Nyen. No: the correct objective was not monopoly but a buoyant revenue, to be achieved by the enlightened exploitation of a favourable middleman position. This, of course, had been the traditional policy of the old Hanseatic towns of the inner Baltic: it was in an effort to break through their entrenched position that Ivan IV had launched his

[1] Soom, 'Die merkantilistische Wirtschaftspolitik Schwedens', p. 202.
[2] *Ibid.*, p. 205.
[3] Almquist, *Kommerskollegium*, pp. 51–2.
[4] For Oxenstierna's economic ideas see *AOSB* I.xi.189; Odhner, *Sveriges inre historia*, pp. 261–6; Boëthius and Heckscher, *Svensk handelsstatistik 1637–1737*, pp. xvii–xviii; Soom, 'Die merkantilistische Wirtschaftspolitik Schwedens', *passim*.

attack upon Livonia a century before. Sweden was doing no more than to apply, on a grander scale, commercial practices which had long been pursued by individual members of the imperial community, though she was backing the application by much more formidable military and naval resources than the Hanse had been able to command. The ports of the provinces thus became the beneficiaries of Sweden's political successes. Already in 1617 Reval and Narva had been accorded, by the Trade Ordinance of that year, staple-rights which put them on a level with the most favoured Swedish towns. It was one of the provisions of the peace of Brömsebro that provincial ports, like the ports of Sweden and Finland, should be exempt from payment of toll at the Sound: in this crucial respect the empire was now treated as a single entity.[1]

The same was true of shipping. The ordinance of 1645 established two categories of Swedish ships, which received preferences equivalent to one-third or one-sixth of the ordinary duty, provided that they were home-built and Swedish-manned; and this preference was from 1652 extended to the provinces also.[2] At first they got little good by it, since so few ships belonged to provincial ports: one of the problems of the imperial power was to persuade Riga and Reval to abandon their long tradition of a 'passive' trade, and to embark on an 'active' trade on their own account in their own ships. But the English Navigation Acts seem – not only for Sweden, but for the provinces also – to have had a stimulating effect in this respect,[3] and that effect was powerfully reinforced by the second and third Anglo-Dutch wars, which offered golden opportunities to neutrals to annex a large share of the Dutch freight-trade: the Swedish yards could not turn out ships fast enough, and local building had to be supplemented by the purchase of Dutch ships, often bought with Dutch money.[4] In this boom the provinces had a modest share; a conspicuous example being the port of Stade. The war with Denmark in the

[1] Sverges traktater med främmande magter, V₂, p. 599.
[2] For this see Birger Fahlborg, 'Ett blad ur den svenska handelsflottans historia (1660–1675)', HT 1923. The ordinance of 1645 is printed in Stiernman, Samling utaf Bref...angående...Commerce, II, pp. 400–14.
[3] Sven Grauers, 'Sverige och den första engelska navigationsakten', in Historiska studier tillägnade Ludwig Stavenow (Stockholm 1924).
[4] Fahlborg, 'Den svenska handelsflottans historia', p. 219.

late seventies caused a recession; but by the nineties Sweden had a respectable mercantile marine; the greater part of the exports from the Baltic region to England were now carried in Swedish ships; and even the burghers of Riga, who in 1623 had not owned a single vessel, had some tonnage to their credit.[1]

In regard to intra-imperial traffic there was less progress: customs-barriers continued to divide province from province, and the empire from the metropole; but even here the imperial connexion was given some recognition, and trade with the provinces was specially privileged as compared with trade to foreign countries.[2] Since the control of tariff policies was in the hands of the College of Commerce, which fixed the customs dues for all the provinces, it might have been expected that this would have acted as a unifying agent. In practice, however, a uniform and self-consistent tariff for the whole empire proved impossible to attain. In the first place, economic regulations were always liable to be modified and upset in response to local military needs, or as a result of purely political considerations. Supplies of grain or potash might be commandeered for the armies, as in 1676, or diverted to threatened allies such as Holstein–Gottorp;[3] or in a period of scarcity the export of grain might be prohibited altogether, to the loss of the producers and the upsetting of the markets.[4] Fiscal policy was liable to be disturbed by a sudden demand for cash, so that in place of the normal, long-term strategy of keeping the rate of duty low, the Stockholm government would raise it abruptly in order to obtain a quick return. There were, moreover, local duties over which Stockholm had no control: Riga, for instance, could in virtue of her privileges levy harbour-dues of her own, which on occasion could amount to three times as much as the imperial customs-dues.[5] Sweden inherited the trading jealousies and commercial rivalries which

---

[1] Liljedahl, *Svensk förvaltning i Livland*, p. 103; S.-E. Åström, *From Stockholm to St Petersburg* (Helsinki 1962), p. 15; Carlson, *Sveriges historia*, v, p. 105 (but contrast *ibid.*, p. 70 and *n* 1).

[2] Heckscher, *Sveriges ekonomiska historia*, II, pp. 657–67, where he writes: 'In comparison with what happened in almost all other countries at that time the Swedish customs system represented an unusually strongly applied unification.'

[3] A. Soom, *Der Baltische Getreidehandel im 17. Jahrhundert* (Stockholm 1961), p. 299.

[4] For examples, see *ibid., passim.*

[5] Wittrock, *Karl XI:s förmyndares finansförvaltning*, II, p. 385.

had for centuries poisoned the relationships of the Baltic towns; of which one example was the long-standing competition of Riga and Dorpat for the trade of Pskov,[1] and another (more recent) the struggle of Reval and Narva for the Russia trade by way of the Gulf of Finland.[2] Upon some of these conflicts the imperial power was able to impose a solution; but others remained intractable. Riga and Reval, for instance, might have different rates of duty; the policy of open access to foreign traders might be negated by the maintenance in certain towns of the old right of emporium: Sweden overrode that right in Reval and Narva (which was one reason for Narva's prosperity), but did not dare to touch it in Riga.[3] Hence it was that in 1662 the nobility of Livonia were forbidden to sell their agricultural produce directly to foreign merchants, while their colleagues in Estonia might have that liberty for six months in the year, and those of Ingria were entirely free of restrictions.[4] Again, differences in the level of economic development might make imperial policies impossible to enforce: the prohibition upon imports of manufactured goods could not be applied to the Baltic provinces since there was no native industry to supply their place.[5] On the other hand, the expulsion of foreign merchants from Sweden in 1696 did not extend to Narva, since to have enforced it would have ruined the trade of the town: nowhere else in the Swedish dominions, it was said, could so many languages be heard in one place.[6]

If, then, the empire was only imperfectly united by the commercial policies of the government, neither was it bound together by any very strong intra-imperial economic ties. Trade between Sweden and the overseas territories was of minor importance before the last two decades of the century. In earlier years imports from the provinces had been mainly the agricultural produce of the great Baltic *latifundia*, which the nobles to whom

---

[1] G. Jenš, 'Rivalry between Riga and Tartu for the trade with Pskov in the XVI and XVII centuries', in *Baltic and Scandinavian Countries*, IV (1938); Liljedahl, *Svensk förvaltning i Livland*, pp. 467–8.

[2] A. Soom, 'De ingermanländska städerna och freden i Stolbova 1617', *Svio-Estonica* 1936.   [3] Nyström, '*Mercatura ruthenica*', pp. 280–3.

[4] Soom, 'Die merkantilistische Wirtschaftspolitik Schwedens', p. 196.

[5] Carlson, *Sveriges historia*, V, pp. 100–1, 104.

[6] Åström, *From Stockholm to St Petersburg*, pp. 74–81; Sigurd Schartau, 'De svenska östersjöprovinserna vid det stora nordiska krigets utbrott. I. Livland', *KFÅ* 1925, pp. 70–1.

they had been donated brought over in their own ships (and sometimes through their private free-ports) for personal consumption, or for marketing at home, or simply to provide a premonitory whiff of the laggard Swedish spring: in at least two instances consignments of lilies of the valley were shipped from Estonia to absentee Swedish landlords.[1] In the eighties, however, the picture changes. Grain exports to Sweden were stimulated by the fall in prices in western Europe which set in after the mid-sixties; but above all by increased Swedish demand.[2] The eighties were years of harvest-failure and stringency, culminating in the famine of 1696–7. In 1685, 13% of Stockholm's imports came from the Baltic provinces, and more than 5% from the German lands.[3] In 1689 Sweden and Finland together took more than half of Reval's grain exports.[4] In 1696 consignments of grain from the empire reached 800,000 tons, which was nearly three times as much as twenty years earlier.[5] In 1700 the mobilization of the Swedish armies was essentially dependent upon supplies of Estonian rye.[6] There was a marked increase in exports also: by 1696 nearly a fifth of Sweden's iron exports went to the overseas provinces.[7] Quite suddenly the Baltic provinces assumed a new importance: they had become Sweden's granary, as necessary to her as Sicily was to Spain. This became very clear when they were devastated by the Russians in 1702 and 1703: in 1704 Fabian Wrede said that without them Sweden could hardly supply herself.[8] Thus just at the moment when (as we shall see) for the first time since the days of Johan Skytte a determined attempt was being made at a real unification of the empire, the provinces began to be linked economically as never before to the metropolitan power.

But it was no more than a beginning. The empire never

---

[1] Arnold Soom, 'Varutransporterna mellan Sverige och de svenskägda baltiska gårdarna under 1600-talet', *Svio-Estonica* 1967, pp. 59, 75.

[2] *Ibid.*, p. 52.

[3] Heckscher, *Sveriges ekonomiska historia*, II, p. 475. Åström estimated the total value of foodstuffs imported from the empire in 1685 at perhaps 300,000 *rdr*: Åström, 'The Swedish Economy', p. 70.   [4] Attman, *Russian and Polish Markets*, p. 41.

[5] Soom, *Der Baltische Getreidehandel*, pp. 75, 281–2.

[6] Cavallie, *Från fred till krig*, p. 231.

[7] Heckscher, *Sveriges ekonomiska historia*, II, p. 475.

[8] Soom, *Der Baltische Getreidehandel*, p. 71; Heckscher, *Sveriges ekonomiska historia*, II, p. 434. Already in 1685 grain represented 12.6% of Stockholm's total imports: *ibid.*, II, p. 552.

developed the same strong economic ties as those which bound Liverpool and Bristol to the Thirteen Colonies and the West Indies, still less the more formalized links which united New and Old Spain, or the province of Holland with the East Indies. No doubt Swedish capital was invested in the empire, in that the great Swedish landowners there put money into improving their estates, or spent it on prestige building:[1] this was certainly true of Jakob and Magnus de la Gardie, both of whom seem to have managed their Estonian properties with great energy and success, and both of whom felt it due to themselves to build on a scale of grandeur appropriate to their exalted social position. The same was true, as far as building was concerned, of Karl-Gustaf Wrangel in Pomerania. To some extent, then, these overseas estates can be regarded as analogues to West Indian plantations. As to how much of the necessary capital was imported from Sweden is another question:[2] it is more likely to have been provided out of local surpluses, or in the form of labour services. Sweden herself suffered from a shortage of domestic capital which does not begin to be overcome before the last third of the century; and for the handful of Swedish *entrepreneurs*, or the great landed magnates such as Magnus Gabriel de la Gardie, there were opportunities for investment nearer home (not least in shipping) without adventuring their money in (say) the trade in flax and hemp of which Riga was the centre. Certainly there seems to have been nothing like a 'colonial interest' in Swedish politics analogous to the West and East India interests at Westminster and The Hague.

Nevertheless, from a narrowly economic point of view, it seems likely that the Baltic provinces gained rather than lost from Swedish rule. That they suffered severely from being involved in Sweden's wars cannot be denied: as far as Livonia was concerned,

---

[1] For the de la Gardies as estate-managers, see Soom, 'Varutransporterna', pp. 68ff. For their building activity, Sten Karling, 'Jakob och Magnus de la Gardie som byggherrar i Estland', *Svio-Estonica* 1938, and Göran Landahl, *Magnus Gabriel de la Gardie, hans gods och hans folk* (Stockholm 1968), pp. 28–30. For Wrangel's building activity in Pomerania, see Gerhard Eimer, *Carl Gustaf Wrangel som byggherre i Pommern och Sverige* (Stockholm 1961).

[2] Hans Wachtmeister had 96,000 d.s.m. invested in Riga in 1700. But on the outbreak of war he took care to transfer it as quickly as possible to Amsterdam: Cavallie, *Från fred till krig*, p. 129.

that rule began and ended in devastation, and the damage inflicted in the fifties as a result of Charles X's wars was just as bad. But on the other hand there is little doubt that agriculture became more productive under Swedish landlords, who brought enlarged areas under cultivation in response to the opportunities presented by the high price of grainstuffs. The trade of the provinces throve under the protective shield of the Swedish navy. Their mercantile marine was coaxed into existence by the advantages opened to it through inclusion in Swedish shipping policy. The increased ease of access to the Russian markets which was afforded by the terms of the treaties of Stolbova and Kardis was a natural *desideratum* for them also. The foundation of Nyen in 1632 for the first time opened the Neva route to western merchants. Swedish attempts to expand the limits of Livonia, and thus to deepen Riga's hinterland towards the middle Düna, Swedish attempts to stifle any competition from Windau and Libau, were directly in Riga's interest. It was no wonder if, despite occasional vexatious interferences with trade for temporary political or military ends, Riga, Narva, and even Reval, ended the century in a flourishing condition.[1] Riga, in particular, may be said to have been pampered: Sweden could not afford to antagonize so important a source of revenue.[2] No doubt it was the realization that they were well off which animated Riga's burghers to such a stout resistance to the Russian onslaught in Charles XII's time. Of the German ports, Stettin – the object of such bitter contention with Brandenburg – failed to realize the hopes which Oxenstierna had entertained of it, for the Great Elector's construction of the Frederick William Canal diverted the Oder trade and left Stettin stranded. Stade, despite a boom in the sixties, remained overshadowed by Bremen.

All in all, then, the conclusion emerges that economic interests did to a considerable extent help to keep the empire together, even

[1] J. Rosén, *Det karolinska skedet* (Lund 1963), pp. 265–6; K.-G. Hildebrand, 'Ekonomiska syften i svensk expansionspolitik 1700–1709', *KFÅ* 1949, pp. 10–15. Reval's prosperity (unlike Riga's) was based on grain imported from its immediate hinterland, and to the end its burghers seem to have been content to drive a passive trade: Arnold Soom, *Der Handel Rigas im 17. Jahrhundert* (Wiesbaden 1969), p. 189.
[2] See, e.g., Wittrock, *Karl XI:s förmyndares finanspolitik*, II, p. 120; Meurling, *Svensk domstolsförvaltning i Livland*, p. 14. Riga was even permitted to exercise minting-rights in alternate years: Wittrock, *Karl XI:s förmyndares finanspolitik*, I, p. 224.

if those interests had not been the motive force behind its acquisition. The commercial policies which Sweden pursued not merely did not contradict the wishes of the provinces, but actually harmonized with them fairly closely; and so gave them an interest, greater than might have been expected, in maintaining the Swedish connexion.

It may well be that economic interests would have remained to the end the strongest unifying force within the empire, had it not been for the political revolution which in the years after 1680 transformed Sweden into a parliamentary absolutism. That revolution, however, had immediate consequences in the field of imperial policy. It brought with it an abrupt return to the ideals and objectives of an earlier day; it made possible the revival of a programme of uniformity; it opened the way to effective reform of social evils.

The definitive acquisition of Skåne, Blekinge, Halland and Bohuslän in 1660 had already forced Sweden to face the question of uniformity afresh, since for these provinces it was an issue which could hardly be evaded. They were direct territorial extensions of the old kingdom, as Wales and Scotland were of England: for them, at least, the old laissez-faire attitude which had done duty for a policy since the early thirties no longer sufficed. If they were to be firmly held against Danish attempts at reconquest, their populations must be fully integrated into the Swedish kingdom, must somehow be reconciled to Swedish rule, and must be made Swedish in language, law and social habits.[1] As early as 1662 they were given representation in the riksdag, and a member of the local nobility entered the Council of State. The University of Lund was founded in 1668 to provide a Swedish academy more accessible than distant Uppsala, or Pomeranian Greifswald. But before 1679 the policy of uniformity was not pressed: Danish law for the time remained,[2] the Danish clergy were left to conduct their services in the old way and in their own language. In the delicate question as to the adjustment of the privileges of the local nobility to Swedish models it even seemed possible for a time that a solution

---

[1] The best short account of the denationalizing process is in Rosén, *Det karolinska skedet*, pp. 70–8, 214–29. And see Alf Åberg, *När Skåne blev svenskt* (Stockholm 1958).

[2] It was, indeed, guaranteed by the treaty of Copenhagen which ceded the provinces to Sweden.

might be found, not in curtailing Danish excesses, but in raising Swedish privileges to the Danish level.

But the experiences of the war of 1675–9 made a firmer and more resolute programme inevitable. The hope of a Danish victory had unloosed formidable guerrilla movements, involving all classes of the population, which had been suppressed only by measures of drastic severity. Compromise, it was clear, would no longer serve: what was required was full incorporation, uniformity in all fields, and total Swedification. Swedish nobles and peasants were accordingly encouraged to settle in the southern provinces; a new, all-Swedish town was established at Karlshamn; and a programme of road-building in the manner of General Wade helped to pacify the areas in which the guerrillas had been accustomed to find refuge.[1] The right to representation in the *riksdag* had been revoked in 1679, and as the price of its restoration the crown now exacted acceptance of its denationalizing measures. They were carried through with surprisingly little resistance, thanks to the tact and firmness of the Governor-General, Rutger von Ascheberg, and the remorseless zeal of the local bishop, Canutus Hahn:[2] the clergy first, the burghers afterwards, were induced to petition the king for Swedish law and Swedish ecclesiastical organization; the Swedish language was inculcated into the younger generation from the pulpit, in catechism classes, and at school. It was a social revolution by extorted consent; and its success was astonishingly swift and enduring. Though doubts were still expressed in Charles XII's time about the loyalty of Skåne, there were already Skånska cavalry regiments in his army.[3] To this day the Skåning may feel himself in some respects more attuned to Copenhagen than to Stockholm, but by the time the Great Northern War was over there was no longer any question but that the former Danish provinces were permanently integrated into the Swedish state.[4]

[1] Alf Åberg, *Rutger von Ascheberg* (Malmö 1950), pp. 187–90; Jerker Rosén, 'Rutger v. Aschebergs ämbetsberättelse 1693', *Scandia* 1946, p. 36 and *passim*.
[2] Åberg, *Rutger von Ascheberg*; G. Göransson, *Canutus Hahn. En biografisk studie* (Lund 1950).
[3] *SRARP* xvii, 279 (12 May 1714); Åberg, *Rutger von Ascheberg*, pp. 262–3.
[4] Though in 1714 Jesper Swedberg, after a visit to Charles XII's headquarters in Skåne, could write afterwards of 'coming home to Sweden': *Jesper Swedbergs Lefwernes Beskrifning*, ed. Gunnar Westerberg (Lund 1941), I, p. 569.

The special problem of Skåne, and the success of the measures taken for dealing with it, may well have contributed to the revival of long-dormant plans for uniformity elsewhere. However that may be, the coming of absolutism after 1680 gave them a decisive impetus.[1] It is significant, for instance, that it was just in the 1680s and 1690s that there were signs of such a policy in Finland, in the shape of attempts to discriminate against the Finnish language, and to restrict its use for official purposes.[2] But it was in the Baltic provinces, and above all in Livonia, that the return to the attitudes of Charles IX and Skytte was most evident. And here, the policy was launched under auspices much more favourable than at any previous epoch. For the power of the crown to impose its will upon recalcitrant corporations was just at this moment enormously strengthened by the operation of the *reduktion*.

In more than one respect the *reduktion* transformed the imperial situation. It was carried out in all the overseas provinces, German as well as Baltic; in all of them any lands once held by the crown, and donated by it on almost any terms, were reduced, and were declared henceforth to be inalienable. The *riksdag* resolutions of 1655 and 1680 laid it down that the *reduktion* should be carried out in the provinces 'according to the nature and character' of each; which meant in fact that in the German lands regard had to be paid to the law of the Empire, and that in all the provinces it must respect such established privileges and constitutional rights as were able to withstand the interpretative ingenuity and sophisticated historical research of the king's legists and archivists. But though Estates or *lantdag* might remonstrate or protest, in fact it was everywhere imposed by royal commissioners, though on terms which varied from province to province.[3] The first donations to be reduced were the great counties and baronies – those vast estates which had occupied so much of the Livonian

[1] Erik Lindschöld, for instance, was a thoroughgoing champion of uniformity: Ola Lindqvist, *Jakob Gyllenborg och reduktionen* (Lund 1946), pp. 152–3.
[2] Pentti Renvall, *Finsk representation i Sveriges riksdag* (Stockholm 1967), p. 177.
[3] For the *reduktion* in Estonia, see Aleksandr Loit, *Kampen om feodalräntan. Reduktion och domänpolitik i Estland 1655–1710* (Uppsala 1975); for Livonia, J. Vasar, *Die grosse livländische Güterreduction* (Acta et commentationes universitatis Tartuenis, XX and XXII) (Tartu 1930–1), and Alvin Isberg, *Karl XI och den livländska adeln 1684–1695* (Lund 1953); for Pomerania, von Essen, *Alienationer och reduktioner*, and Malmström, *Nils Bielke*; for Bremen–Verden, Carlson, *Sveriges historia*, III, p. 285; and for a general survey, Rosén, *Det karolinska skedet*, pp. 194–205, 229–32.

landscape; the next, those granted to other Swedish noblemen – who, like the counts and barons, were often enough absentee landlords. The process made a clean sweep of a great vested interest: within a few years the ties which had united Swedish and Baltic nobility in opposition to reform were weakened, though they were not wholly destroyed. The high nobility in Sweden had in any case been so battered into submission by the retributive proceedings against the Regents and the Council that it was no longer in a position to defend its class interests in the provinces against a reforming monarch: at best it could count itself fortunate if it were permitted to retain its Baltic estates as tenants-at-will of the crown; at worst, it lost everything.[1]

Even more far-reaching in its effects was what happened when the *reduktion* was extended, as it very soon was, to the former lands of the crown in the possession of the local Baltic nobility. Some of these donations dated back to long before the territories passed into Swedish hands: in Pomerania, estates were reduced which had been alienated as far back as 1569. The native nobility, which had witnessed with stoicism the dispossession of the Swedish incomers, was touched on the raw when the *reduktion* was applied to what they regarded as their allodial estates. It was not very long before their anger generated serious constitutional conflicts, above all in Livonia. But the crown was no longer to be frightened into concessions by a show of resistance, and it had much less tenderness than of old for privileges, corporations and so-called liberties. With the land in its possession, with the revenues from the land at its disposal, it was determined to enforce its will, and in no bad position for doing so. In Livonia, for instance, the royal revenues rose by more than 25%, and five-sixths of the area of the province reverted to crown ownership.[2] The provinces,

---

[1] The assignment by the crown of these reduced lands as sources of income to pay the salaries of members of the king's Council did however restore the old connexion to some extent; though (as J. G. Stenbock was to find) the income might be inconveniently difficult to realize: A. Kullberg, *Johan Gabriel Stenbock och reduktionen* (Uppsala 1973), pp. 129, 132; and see Carlson's comment, *Sveriges historia*, v, p. 140.

[2] Alvin Isberg, *Karl XI och den livländska adeln 1684–1695* (Lund 1953), p. 86; J. Vasar, 'Om Karl XI:s bondereformer i Livland', *Svio-Estonica 1934*, p. 88. The *reduktion* was accompanied by a cadastral survey of the territorial fiscal units (*Haken*) which increased the number of taxable peasant farms by about a quarter: Edgars Dunsdorfs, *Der grosse schwedische Kataster in Livland, 1681–1710* (Stockholm 1950), p. 188. In Estonia, more than half the land in the province was reduced: Loit, *Kampen om feodalräntan*, p. 312.

indeed, contributed a disproportionately large share of the total gains of the *reduktion*: if the German and Baltic territories are lumped together, rather more than 60% of the whole.[1] The effect of this was to revolutionize the imperial financial situation. When the *reduktion* was complete, as it virtually was by 1700, the old problem of the self-sufficiency of the provinces was found to have disappeared. They were now not merely self-supporting; they had a substantial surplus to contribute to the Treasury in Stockholm:[2] for the first time the empire ran at a profit.

The passing of the greater part of the land into the king's hands had other consequences also. It made possible, for instance, a policy of social reform. The crown was now the ecclesiastical patron of the great majority of parishes: the presentation to livings on all reduced estates was henceforward (as in Sweden) in the king's hands. He was therefore in a position to secure the institution of godly ministers conversant with the languages of their congregations; and there was some hope of securing that they should receive a decent provision. The Church Law of 1686, which had been drawn up by civil servants and imposed upon Sweden by royal authority, became the law for the whole empire. The long-drawn battle of Reval to obtain recognition of its pretension to the *jus episcopale* now ended in final defeat.[3] The crown used its ascendancy to embark upon a massive programme of primary education in the Baltic languages; and before Charles XI's reign was ended, almost every parish in Livonia had been provided with some sort of a school.[4] At long last the Bible was translated into Lettish; and in 1693 Reval received its first native-born bishop.[5]

[1] Heckscher, *Sveriges ekonomiska historia*, II, p. 425: 1.3 million *d.s.m.* out of an estimated total of 2 million; Rosén, *Det karolinska skedet*, p. 205.

[2] Heckscher, *Sveriges ekonomiska historia*, II, p. 424. In 1699 the revenue of Sweden–Finland amounted to 4.17 million *d.s.m.*; that of the Baltic provinces to 1.38 million, and of the German provinces to 1.03 million. Of the total of 2.41 million from the provinces, pehaps 1.2 million went to objects outside them. Cavallie (*Från fred till krig*, pp. 20, 23) gives slightly lower figures for the provinces' revenues; Lundkvist ('An Experience of Empire', pp. 23–4) estimates that 'a good 10%' of the Swedish budget came from surpluses in the Baltic lands. There were no contributions to the Swedish exchequer from the German provinces: Cavallie, *Från fred till krig*, p. 24.

[3] For church reform in Estonia, Isberg, *Kyrkoförvaltningsproblem i Estland*, pp. 155–72, 179–82.

[4] Schartau, 'De svenska östersjöprovinserna, I', p. 23. In Estonia only a beginning was made: Isberg, *Kyrkoförvaltningsproblem i Estland*, p. 174; Schartau, 'De svenska östersjöprovinserna, II', p. 7.

[5] Isberg, *Kyrkoförvaltningsproblem i Estland*, p. 173.

At the same time the University of Dorpat, which had been
defunct since the Russian invasions of Charles X's time, was put
on its legs again, its curriculum was modernized, and it was
provided with a staff of some distinction.[1] All aspirants to
positions in the local civil service were now required to have
studied at Dorpat for at least two years. The University was still
regarded with suspicion by the local nobility as an instrument of
Swedish propaganda; but though there may be some doubt as to
how far the suspicion was justified, it was certainly hostile to
German–Balt influences, and it drew a majority of its undergraduates after its restoration from the Lettish and Estonian
populations.[2]

One of the great obstacles in the way of religious reformation
had always been the institution of serfdom; and the attempts to
have it modified or abolished had in part derived as much from
concern for the spiritual as for the material welfare of the
peasantry: the burden of labour services made it impossible for
them to come to church. But for the Church it was of course also
a matter of economics. The peasantry must be in a position to pay
tithe; it must not bury its dead in the nearest bog in order to escape
paying burial-fees. The clash between Rudbeckius and the
Estonian nobility had from one point of view been simply an
extension of a running battle with the nobility – on tithe, on the
right of presentation – which was in full swing in Sweden itself.
The Church too, in this respect, was a 'corporation' in the
Estonian sense, and it had been as careful of its interests as any
other. In contrast with the position in Sweden, the clergy had little
in common with their flocks, felt themselves socially far above
them, did not feel called upon to champion their cause, and indeed
often treated them with the indifferent brutality of the Baltic
nobility.[3] 'Esthiae bestiae', as a Swedish commissioner had once
remarked; and the parson's job was not to ameliorate their
condition in this world, but to provide them with a properly
visa'd Protestant passport to the next. In 1692 one of the clergy's
difficulties was settled by an ordinance which commanded that

[1] G. von Rauch, 'Naturrätten vid Dorpts akademi. Ett bidrag till kännedomen om
1600-talets andliga strömningar i det svenska Livland', Svio-Estonica 1936, pp. 51–73.
[2] Isberg, Karl XI, p. 185; Rosén, Det karolinska skedet, p. 233.
[3] Alvin Isberg, 'Livländska prästmän inför överkonsistoriets domareskrank', Svio-
Estonica 1967, p. 33.

all peasants be free from work between 4 o'clock on Saturday afternoons and Monday morning.[1] But it was not only the religious aspect of the problem that concerned Charles XI and his ministers: they objected to serfdom on principle. Bengt Oxenstierna, for instance, compared the Baltic nobility's treatment of their peasants with the Spaniards' treatment of the American Indians.[2] It was undoubtedly Charles XI's wish to sweep away serfdom altogether, and for lands reduced to the crown it did in fact come to an end, though never formally abolished. As to lands still held by the nobility, he contented himself with forbidding 'harsh and improper treatment', arbitrary corporal punishment, and private prisons.[3] But like his predecessors he stopped short of a radical reformation for fear of straining the loyalty of the nobility too far. After 1694, when their breach with the crown became irreparable, this consideration lost much of its force; and if Charles had lived longer, and if the war had not supervened, it seems possible that a general abolition of serfdom might not have been long delayed.[4]

The effect of Swedish efforts to ameliorate the lot of the Baltic peasantry is still a matter of debate among historians, whose judgment depends upon whether they look mainly to what was done, or to what might have been done. On the whole, it seems probable that any benefit from the reforms of the Skytte period was dissipated in the decades of aristocratic predominance which followed.[5] The Swedish landlords very soon adapted themselves to what no doubt were represented to be the facts of life in Livonia, and it seems clear that they treated their peasantry no better than the native nobility.[6] It is significant that the flight of peasants over the frontier into Russia was a perennial problem: as Erik Andersson Trana once put it, 'the peasant sits as lightly

---

[1] Isberg, *Kyrkoförvaltningsproblem i Estland*, pp. 134, 156.

[2] Isberg, *Karl XI*, p. 223.

[3] Schartau, 'De svenska östersjöprovinserna, 1', pp. 7–12.

[4] *Ibid.*, p. 13. For Charles XI and the lot of the peasantry, see Vasar, 'Om Karl XI:s bondereformer', *Svio-Estonica* 1934; *id.*, 'Utvecklingen av böndernas rättsläge', *Svio-Estonica* 1936.

[5] A. Švābe, *Grundriss der Agrargeschichte Lettlands* (Riga 1928), p. 161; Vasar, 'Utvecklingen av böndernas rättsläge', pp. 27ff.; J. Loit, 'De svenska dagöböndernas kamp för sina fri- och rättigheter 1662–1685', *Svio-Estonica* 1952.

[6] For an example of how Baltic barbarism could infect an otherwise estimable Swedish civil servant, see the case of Georg Stiernhielm and the peasant Peep: P. Wieselgren, *Georg Stiernhielm* (Stockholm 1948), p. 23.

on the frontier as the bird on the bough for the marksman, and
flies away when he will'; and in 1656 the peasantry of Ingria
deserted *en masse* to the invading Russian armies.[1] The immediate
effect of the *reduktion* in Livonia seems, contrary to what might
have been expected, to have been an actual worsening of the
peasants' lot; for the king believed (quite rightly) that the
maximum advantage to the exchequer could be obtained by
leasing the vast reduced estates to their previous owners, rather
than by managing them through royal bailiffs.[2] The result was
that they tended to be run by agents who had little previous
connexion with them, and were often of urban origin; and the
local royal administration in the province was too new, too thin
on the ground, and at first too inadequately organized, to be able
to check the resulting abuses. In 1683 there were mass flights of
peasants, many of whom went over to Stockholm to petition the
king. They did not go in vain. Charles XI took stringent measures
to set right what was amiss: on the whole, with success.[3] A final
verdict on the fate of the peasants must await the publication of
Dr Loit's second volume; but even Baltic historians are prepared
to concede that Charles's reign brought great changes for the
better, though some of them are inclined to ascribe them to purely
fiscal motives. But this, perhaps, is unjust. There was a genuine
tradition of idealism, spanning the century from Charles IX to
Charles XI, a feeling of responsibility and concern, a belief in
Swedish values and standards; a tradition which was also anti-
aristocratic. It was for long necessary for the upholders of that
tradition to compromise with political expediency: absolutes were
conceivable only to an absolutism, and even then proved
unattainable; but what was important was that the attempt was
made and persisted in. It does not appear that any Livonian serf
ever escaped to Sweden and claimed his freedom there; but if the
issue in *Somerset's Case* had ever come before Charles XI, it is a
fair guess that his verdict would have coincided with Lord
Mansfield's.

Now that the crown had most of the land in its hands, it had

[1] Liljedahl, *Svensk förvaltning i Livland*, pp. 529–30; Carlson, *Sveriges historia*, I,
pp. 32–3.
[2] Loit, *Kampen om feodalräntan*, ch. VII: Loit's argument on this point, though it
concerns Estonia, is applicable also to Livonia.
[3] Vasar, 'Om Karl XI:s bondereformer', pp. 91–3; Soom, 'Varutransporterna',
p. 80; Lundkvist, 'An Experience of Empire', pp. 43–4.

a natural interest in regulating its business by the principles and forms of Swedish law. That law was now applied more effectively than ever before: for the first time it was imposed on Riga; in 1690 it was ordered to be used even in local courts in Livonia; in 1694 Swedish civil law was prescribed for Estonia; though in each case with modifications necessary to accommodate some local peculiarities.[1] The change was very much for the better. Whereas in Sweden torture had never had legal sanction, in Livonia (significantly enough) it had been expressly legalized in 1632. But now in 1686 Charles XI prohibited its use in all his dominions.[2] It must be a matter of regret that Sweden had to wait for a century, and for the coming of another enlightened despot, before the ordinary citizen could be sure that the prohibition would not be flouted by the sovereign Estates in the name of 'Swedish liberties'.

Meanwhile 'Livonian liberties' – if by that name we can dignify the vested interests of the local *Junkertum* – received short shrift. Deeply alienated by the *reduktion*, sore and suspicious at Charles's reforms, they found in Patkul a leader who was able to throw a specious cloak of 'patriotism' over crass class-interest.[3] The rupture with the Livonian nobility, which became final in 1694, gave the absolutism a chance to stifle the old organs of aristocratic self-government. The institution of the *lantråd* was swept away, the *lantdag* ceased to function: the Governor-General even suggested that it be abolished, and Livonia be joined to Sweden in a parliamentary union. But even among the devoted servants of the absolutism there survived aristocratic traditions strong enough to block this proposal; and just as Axel Oxenstierna had rejected incorporation in 1643, so Bengt Oxenstierna persuaded his sovereign to reject it in 1694 – and upon not dissimilar grounds.[4]

[1] Meurling, *Svensk domstolsförvaltning i Livland*, pp. 80, 212, 234, 243, 254–8, 261, 270.

[2] H. Munktell, 'Tortyren i svensk rättshistoria. Ett bidrag till straffprocessrättens historia', *Lychnos* 1939, 1940, pp. 131, 145–6.

[3] For Patkul, see Isberg, *Karl XI*, pp. 108–18, 193–201, 225–56; *id.*, 'Johann Reinhold Patkul och Livland åren 1699–1701', *KFÅ* 1960; *id.*, 'Johan Reinhold Patkuls politiska handlande. En historisk skiss', *KFÅ* 1967; R. Liljedahl, 'Östersjöprovinsernas svenska tid i den tysk-baltiska historieskrivningen', *HT* 1929, pp. 205, 213–22.

[4] Isberg, *Karl XI*, pp. 286–9; Carlson, *Sveriges historia*, v, p. 177; Meurling, *Svensk domstolsförvaltning i Livland*, p. 34.

So the empire confronted its last great struggle with only the incorporation of the former Danish provinces effected. But though the integration of the others had proved impracticable (and for some of them had never even been contemplated), the last two decades of the century had seen long strides towards uniformity: not, indeed, in the German lands, where even the absolutism took care not to upset existing constitutional compromises, but certainly in the Baltic provinces. At the end, as in the beginning, we can discern a positive imperial policy, now applied more forcefully and more successfully than ever before.[1] When Charles XI's life was cut short, he left behind him an empire which was at least beginning to be something more than a geographical expression, or the *ex post facto* construct of a historian. Much done; much more to do; but signs, at least, that much more was intended.

How far an imperial policy had any meaning for the average Swede – how far the *riksdag*, for instance, thought of the empire as anything but an expensive bulwark, how far it was an object of national pride – may well be doubted. It does not seem that it ever captured men's imaginations: certainly it offered neither the exotic nor the financial attractions of the Indies. The government of the empire was too decentralized for the *riksdag* to have much concern with it. It is striking how rarely imperial issues came up for discussion at its meetings. To the Estate of Peasants the empire was of interest only as a dreadful warning of the social and political degradation which might overtake them if the alienation of crown land to the nobility continued: the danger of 'a Livonian servitude' in Sweden, real or imagined (and the most recent research tends to suggest that it was less imminent than used to be thought) was a staple item in their *gravamina* at *riksdag* after *riksdag*, and a useful propaganda-line when they wished to appeal to the crown or to rally the support of the other non-noble Estates. The Estate of Clergy, for its part, was concerned with the empire mainly because it had from time to time to resolve the disputes of cantankerous provincial churchmen. For the Estate of Nobility, on the other hand, the empire presented problems of a domestic nature. They spent a good deal of time in debating,

[1] For a clear statement of the policy of uniformity, see the Proposition to the *riksdag* of 1697: *SRARP* XVI.292.

with appropriate thoroughness, the qualifications of provincials to be admitted to membership of the *Riddarhus*: were the sons of Ingrian boyars, for instance, to be considered as eligible? – a question which (surprisingly enough) they answered in the affirmative: hence the appearance in Swedish annals of such well-known names as Aminoff.[1] But their main concern was in connexion with the *reduktion*; and here their debates followed a pattern which had really nothing to do with attitudes towards the empire. The great majority of the nobility clamoured for the application of the *reduktion* to the provinces to the fullest extent: all former crown lands, they insisted, must be held to be reducible, and inalienable for the future. So it was in 1655; so again in 1680. It was in vain that successive *lantmarskalkar* or sober elder statesmen pointed out to them that the provinces had privileges which must be respected; in vain that they were reminded that it had been agreed that the *reduktion* should proceed according to the 'nature and character' of each province: the clamour could not be silenced.[2] Most of the nobility, after all, were in the crown's service, to a considerable extent dependent on salaries and wages which the crown was too poor to pay. Their hope was that a stringent *reduktion* might enable the king to give them their arrears and pay them regularly thereafter; and they were led to expect that it would guarantee them against the levying of those 'contributions' which in fact infringed their fiscal immunities, and which they bitterly resented. In the overseas provinces they had for the most part no territorial or financial interest whatever. They might on occasion, as an act of piety, be prepared to make a trifling contribution towards restoring a church in Narva or Stettin;[3] but for them the empire appeared as the lush pasture of a small *élite* whose social pretensions they resented, and whose ostentatious luxury aroused their jealousy. They would not leave such persons an acre of land in Livonia, if as a consequence the ordinary nobleman must once again put his hand into his pocket. 'What has it profited us here in Sweden', they cried, 'that we helped to conquer the country?

---

[1] *SRARP* x.260, 290–2, 363; xvi.28, 265–6. The crown on occasion seems to have put pressure on them to infringe the provision in the Form of Government debarring non-residents from being admitted: *cf.* Soom, 'Die merkantilistische Wirtschaftspolitik Schwedens', p. 192.

[2] *SRARP* v₂.117–19, 198, 304; viii.134; x.338; xi.132, 134–9; xiii.73, 82–3, 139–54, 168–70, 349.   [4] *SRARP* viii.131; xiii.198.

In such a case our lot is harder than that of the Livonians.'[1] As it happened, they need not have excited themselves: Charles XI made a clean sweep of Livonian donations; but the 'contribution' continued to be exacted just the same. The high nobility, the great Council families, naturally enough took the other line: it was from their ranks, and from theirs alone, that were drawn the holders of those donations which covered so great a portion of the Baltic lands, and which the *reduktion* immediately threatened. Thus in the period between 1655 and 1682 imperial policy became a not unimportant aspect of the fierce contentions which divided the first Estate, and which paved the way for the absolutism.

This, however, was an exceptional situation. Despite the broad lands won by the Swedish sword, despite Sweden's sudden move into Europe, the Swedes of the Age of Greatness remained at heart inward-looking, and pride of empire made no part of the national *ethos*. To those with overseas estates, those with cadet lines established in the provinces, no doubt the empire had real importance: in 1710 Fabian Wrede alleged that the Russian conquest of Livonia had cost him 3,000 *rdr* a year;[2] and the peace of Nystad would for many of them bring a hard choice, and the separation of families. Certainly the empire offered few opportunities to the careerist. To the man of law the Supreme Court at Dorpat, with its low salaries, had little attraction: *auskultanter* were not easy to come by; and one of its presidents, Lars Fleming, was for 22 years an absentee in Sweden.[3] Wismar was perhaps a little better: good enough, at least, to provide a convenient siding into which to shunt that troublesome character Bengt Skytte. As with the law, so with the church: only the hope of using a provincial preferment as a stepping-stone to something better at home could induce an ambitious cleric to accept the low stipend and isolation of a colonial bishopric. The provincial universities of Greifswald and Dorpat were too small to offer many prospects. The government made genuine efforts to do its best for Greifswald – Charles XII even issued ordinances compelling any Swedish undergraduates who wished to go to a German university to make it their first choice. But despite well-meant efforts it refused to thrive: at the end of the century it had only forty students, and

---

[1] *SRARP* xiv.57.　　　　[2] *SRARP* xvii.37.
[3] Meurling, *Svensk domstolsförvaltning i Livland*, p. 64.

its library no more than 800 volumes. Moreover, the government's scrupulous care to respect its ancient privileges ensured that it should remain an essentially alien institution. The Swedish universities suspected it of giving cheap degrees; and no Swede was appointed to a chair until as late as 1708.[1] The German provinces no doubt did something to reinforce the closer association of Sweden with the broad currents of European life which involvement in the Thirty Years War had produced; but the Baltic lands could offer few corresponding benefits: they were something of a cultural dead-end.[2]

If it is difficult to identify any general attitude on the part of Swedes towards the empire, it is no easier to define the attitude of the provinces towards the imperial power. For in truth there was scarcely any attitude common to them all. It is a significant fact that upon the greatest common domestic issue to confront them – the *reduktion* – there is no sign whatever of any attempt to coordinate aristocratic resistance between one province and another: the contrast with the Habsburg lands in 1618, to say nothing of Virginia and Massachusetts, is revealing. Yet for all of them Sweden was, to a modest extent, the land of opportunity, as the long succession of German and Baltic names in the roster of the Swedish nobility testifies. A respectable list could be compiled of prominent figures who, though of provincial origin, made their fortunes and their reputations in Sweden, or in the Swedish service; some thirteen of them succeeded in becoming members of the Council.[3] In 1664 Magnus Gabriel de la Gardie characteristically proposed that 'persons of distinction' in Pomerania and the other provinces be given appointments at Court, in order to polish up their manners and reinforce their loyalty; but four years later Jakob Fleming commented: 'The Romans had many foreign provinces under them; but they admitted no foreigner to attendance at Court.'[4] In eastern Europe, and still more in Germany, the Swedish government relied heavily on recruits from the provinces to conduct its diplomacy. Much more

[1] Seth, *Universitetet i Greifswald*, pp. 102, 108, 124–5, 127, 153–5.

[2] For such reciprocal cultural influences as there were, see Sten Karling, 'Balticum och Sverige', in *Antikvariska studier* III (*Kungl. Vitterhets-Historie- och Antikvitetsakedemiens Handlingar 65*) (Stockholm 1968).

[3] Though of course only after they had become resident in Sweden–Finland. Sjödell, *Riksråd och kungliga råd*, pp. 25–6.

[4] Wittrock, *Karl XI:s förmyndares finanspolitik*, I, p. 227; *SRARP* X.157.

numerous were those who made a career in the army: as the statistics quoted by Professor Lundkvist demonstrate, the Baltic provinces in particular provided a disproportionately high percentage of officers.[1] But in a period when Sweden attracted foreigners of many nationalities – Scots, German, Dutch – it would be easy to make too much of this.

The German provinces had struggled hard to escape Swedish rule; but once it was imposed they seem to have lived under it contentedly enough. This was certainly the case with Pomerania, whose inhabitants very soon felt themselves to be Swedes, and were strongly loyal during Charles XI's war with the Great Elector.[2] They much preferred being a part of the Swedish empire to the prospect of incorporation into Brandenburg: in the first instance, because the Swedish connexion offered better advantages for trade. Even in the later years of Charles XII such discontent as there was seems to have been directed against the burden of war, and not at all against Sweden as such. In the next century the feeling of identity grew stronger rather than weaker; and when in 1806 Gustav IV Adolf by a *coup d'état* suspended the Pomeranian constitution, introduced Swedish law, and abolished serfdom, he became enormously popular with the Pomeranian masses. When at last in 1815 Pomerania passed into Prussian hands, there can be no doubt that the great majority of its inhabitants regretted the change.[3] In the Baltic lands loyalty to Sweden varied from one group of the population to another. The towns, and of course the Swedish colonists in Estonia, clung to the Swedish connexion. The nobility was ready to accept it, if only their class interests and privileges were respected,[4] and in the end Peter the Great gave them what Charles XI had refused. For the peasantry, the answer remains in doubt: the evidence as to their reaction to the Russian invasion after 1700 is conflicting.[5] They seem in fact to have been far more concerned with their immediate material

[1] Lundkvist, 'The Experience of Empire', pp. 54–5.
[2] Claes Rålamb was over-gloomy when at a dark moment in August 1675 he told the Council that one-third of Pomerania had 'gone over' to Brandenburg: *RRP* III Series, NF I, *Stenografiska Protokoll* (Stockholm 1975), p. 270.
[3] Peters, 'Unter der schwedischen Krone', pp. 42–50.
[4] Alvin Isberg, 'Majestätsbrott och landsförrädare i Livland under det karolinska enväldets slutskede', *Svio-Estonica* 1964.
[5] Otto Liiv, 'Folkstämningen i Estland vid början av det stora nordiska kriget', *Svio-Estonica* 1934; Henrik Sepp, 'Estland under det stora nordiska kriget och svenska östproblemet', *Svio-Estonica* 1936.

needs than with the question whether Swedish, German, Russian or Polish was to be the language of their rulers; for all were foreign languages to them. Charles XI's reforms, it seems, came too late to influence them very much. But this at least is clear: in no part of the empire was there anything resembling opposition to Swedish rule on nationalistic grounds. In the next chapter I shall consider the causes of the empire's collapse; but it can immediately be said that it will not do to see it in terms of the overthrow of a hated colonialist *régime*. Whatever else the empire was, it was not a collection of oppressed peoples rightly struggling to be free.

IV

The Unmaking of the Empire

WHEN an empire no longer serves the purposes for which it was created, and has in the meantime discovered no new justification for its existence, it is ripe for its fall. If we are to attempt some explanation of the collapse of the Swedish empire, one useful line of approach may be to enquire how far, in the half-century after 1660, the empire in fact answered the expectations of its architects. This threatens, of course, to bring us back to that controversy between the Old School and the New, discussed in chapter I. But if the New School is right, if the empire was created for the purposes of commercial monopoly, then our question is easily answered. For such a monopoly was never in sight of attainment: Breitenfeld had been fought in vain, the gains of Westphalia were irrelevant decorations, Charles X was merely a portly and unsuccessful *Schreckenberger*. The empire made no sense; and there is no need to protract the discussion beyond this point.

But if the New School has got its proportions wrong? If we assume that the expansion was basically defensive in motivation, that the objective was security, and the means to ensure that that security should be real: what then? From this point of view, the results of Sweden's efforts were undeniably impressive: the outcome seemed to answer the design. They had set bounds to what they called 'Russian barbarism', and shut off Moscow from the sea. They had broken Denmark's absolute control of the Sound, and expanded Sweden's frontiers to their natural limits; and from the new German possessions they posed a threat to Jutland which, it might be hoped, would guarantee them against Danish aggression in the future: Axel Oxenstierna once described Pomerania as 'a rope round the King of Denmark's neck'.[1] The 'Evangelical Cause' in Germany had been saved, in spite of itself,

---

[1] D. Norrman, *Gustav Adolfs politik mot Ryssland och Polen under trettioåriga kriget* (Uppsala 1943), p. 2.

THE SWEDISH EMPIRE, 1660

Narva

Reval

Novgorod

Stockholm

Pskov

Riga

BALTIC SEA

Karlskrona

SWEDISH
POMERANIA

Danzig

Wismar

Hamburg

Bremen

BREMEN-
VERDEN

Stettin

0   500

KILOMETRES

from a destruction which might have been followed by an attack on Scandinavian Protestantism. The crucially important ports of the Baltic – the potential invasion-ports – were now mostly in Swedish hands, Danzig alone excepted. And if war should threaten again, the provinces gave Sweden important advantages which had hitherto been lacking. They provided, for instance, direct access to the German mercenary-market.[1] They furnished mustering-places, outside Sweden proper, for the concentration of forces. They constituted strong bridge-heads, safe places for disembarkation, well-sited launching-pads for an offensive. They greatly eased the financial and logistical problems of mobilization; and they were buffers or bastions to shield Sweden herself from the impact of enemy attack. It might be contended that there were political advantages too, at least from the German provinces. It was their possession which made it possible for Sweden to appear as a great power; and her right to them was entrenched in the Westphalian settlement, of which Sweden was one of the three guarantors. They gave her a seat in three Circles of the Empire; they ensured that her voice should be heard in the affairs of Germany; they asserted the claim of Gustav Adolf's successors to be regarded as *caput* of German Protestantism. That pretension had indeed emerged somewhat tarnished from the reigns of Christina and Charles X; but Swedish diplomacy in the sixties would make it plain that it was still a reality.

It was thus that the creators of the empire viewed their work; it was thus that Axel Oxenstierna viewed it. Not a few Swedish historians have followed that illustrious example. Yet even those who consider that in the long run Sweden's imperial destiny imposed a burden which was too heavy for her to bear do not as a rule make one point which seems to me to emerge with great force from the history of the reign of Charles XI: the point, that is, that if empire-building was designed to provide security, if it was a defensive operation, then it was an operation that failed.

---

[1] Landberg, *Krig på kredit*, p. 6; and *cf.* Böhme, *Bremisch-verdische Staatsfinanzen*, p. 183. When Pomerania was temporarily lost in 1677–8 this had a marked adverse effect upon the ability to recruit mercenaries: C. O. Nordensvan, 'Svenska armén under senare hälften av 1600-talet', *KFÅ* 1923, pp. 24–5. The need for ready access to the mercenary market meant that all powers with any military pretensions must have some sort of stake in Germany – as Harald Hjärne remarked long ago: Hjärne, *Karl XII*, p. 29.

The empire did not give Sweden the security that she sought: on the contrary. No doubt the peace of Stolbova warded off the danger from Russia, as the peace of Copenhagen blunted that from Denmark. But the German provinces made Sweden more, not less, vulnerable. Militarily and politically they brought a threat to security, rather than a reinforcement of it. Since the time of Gustav Vasa, Swedish foreign policy had been dominated by the fear of a war on two fronts. The acquisition of the German provinces meant that henceforward she ran the risk of war, not on two fronts, but on three: and this duly happened, as early as 1659. The defence of the Baltic provinces could count on some help from the facts of geography: rivers and lakes offered water-barriers to an invader. But the German provinces had no such advantages: they lay open to attack; the rivers ran through them, not round them. It was therefore necessary to maintain in Germany considerable mercenary armies, in addition to the Swedish troops which served as garrisons in places of strategic importance.[1] In 1658 Charles X estimated that the defence of Pomerania would require 8,000 men in peacetime and 17,000 in time of war.[2] True, these troops were supposed to cost Sweden nothing, for they were supposed to be borne upon the provincial budgets. But it was also necessary to spend large sums on fortifications – in Pomerania, in particular; and this necessitated substantial contributions from the Swedish taxpayer. This concentration upon defence-works in Pomerania was one factor (though not the only one) which led to a dangerous neglect of the defences of the Baltic provinces. Yet despite the local army, despite the fortifications, Pomerania was lost, in whole or in part, in almost every war in which Sweden engaged after 1648: in 1659, 1677, 1713, 1759, 1808. Twice in this century it was restored to Sweden only by the diplomatic intervention of France. But Pomerania was a kind of symbol: the sign that Sweden was a great European power; and for more than a century and a half her statesmen clung to it because they would not willingly abdicate that position. In 1724 Arvid Horn told the Senate: 'Small though Pomerania is, it nevertheless is more important to our reputation than half Sweden. All the attention which France and the

---

[1] Backhaus, *Reichsterritorium und schwedische Provinz*, p. 142.
[2] *SRARP* VI.300.

Protestant powers in Germany gives to us depends on Pomerania';
and half a century after that, upon the rumour of a plan to offer
Sweden territorial concessions on the Finnish border in return for
the cession of Pomerania to Prussia, Ulrik Scheffer indignantly
rejected the idea, with the comment that it was 'un arrangement
qui nous priverait de la meilleure de nos provinces et nous séparait
du reste de l'Europe'.[1]

Not only had the German provinces long exposed frontiers,
defensible only by fortifications in depth which Sweden could not
afford; they were also highly vulnerable in that they were
dependent upon the Swedish navy for succour if an attack on them
were persisted in. The local armies could at best mount a holding
action: sooner rather than later reinforcements must be sent from
Sweden. But in 1671 Gustaf Kurck reckoned that it might take
as much as seven months to get troops to Bremen;[2] and even a
convoy to Stralsund might be ice-bound in home ports, or driven
back by storms. In regard to the Baltic provinces this was a less
important consideration, for their defence was based on the
calculation that reinforcements could reach them quickly from
Finland overland.

If the military facilities offered by the German provinces proved
to be more than offset by their disadvantages, the same was true
of the political consequences they entailed. The importance of
Bremen–Verden, for instance, was held to be that it provided
Sweden with a power-base in north-west Germany from which
she could exert pressure to maintain the European balance and the
Westphalian settlement, and also that it lay within striking
distance of the Netherlands, and of Denmark.[3] But the only
convenient means of access to it was by land from Pomerania; and
to safeguard that road it was essential to have the friendship of
Holstein–Gottorp. Holstein–Gottorp, in fact, became the keystone
of Sweden's north-German arch; and the strategic importance of
the territory meant that Sweden was politically Gottorp's prisoner:

---

[1] J. F. Schartau, *Hemliga Handlingar hörande till Sveriges historia efter Konung Gustaf III:s Anträde till Regeringen*, III.77 (Stockholm 1822), Ulrik Scheffer to Creutz, 29 October 1771. For Arvid Horn's comment, see Peters, 'Unter der schwedischen Krone', p. 40.
[2] Wittrock, *Karl XI:s förmyndares finanspolitik*, II, p. 289.
[3] See, e.g., Zetterqvist, *Grundläggningen af det svenska väldet*, pp. 9, 70; B. Fahlborg, *Sveriges yttre politik 1664–1668* (Stockholm 1949), I, p. 107.

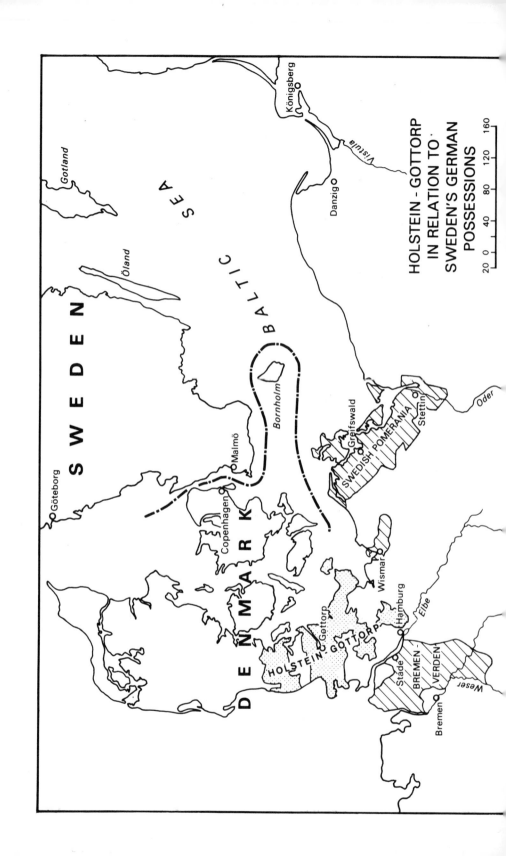

HOLSTEIN - GOTTORP
IN RELATION TO
SWEDEN'S GERMAN
POSSESSIONS

20 0 40 80 120 160

except in the direst emergency,[1] Gottorp *must* be supported. This in turn meant that Danish hostility became unappeasable and perpetual. If Sweden could have afforded to let Gottorp down the history of the later seventeenth century might have taken a very different turn.[2] Again: the possession of the duchy of Bremen led to an attempt to establish Swedish authority over the town of Bremen also. The Westphalian settlement had left the legal position vague, and Sweden had some ground for her pretensions; but the attempt to enforce them antagonized the whole of Germany. Sweden's presence in the Lower Saxon Circle was in itself an offence to (for instance) the Brunswick dukes: its ultimate consequence was Hanover's adherence to the coalition against Charles XII. Already in 1675 the Council was saying that Bremen could not be defended, and Johan Gabriel Stenbock was proposing that it be handed over to England for the duration of the war.[3] Altogether, it might have been better if Charles X had clinched the bargain with Cromwell, and presented him with the duchy in return for financial support.[4]

As to Pomerania, its acquisition brought Sweden another potential enemy which she could well have done without, in the shape of successive Electors of Brandenburg and Kings of Prussia. And to what end? Sweden's possession of Pomerania had been designed to safeguard the Baltic shore, to prevent potential invasion-ports from passing into the hands of any hostile power, and of the Habsburgs in particular. After 1660 that situation, that danger, had in effect ceased to exist. It did indeed seem, for a moment in the sixties, that the Counter-Reformation was on the march again: there was a disturbing little epidemic of conversions among north German princely houses which had hitherto been reliably Protestant. But even the perturbed imaginations of statesmen in Stockholm, troubled with a traditional (but now superfluous) concern for 'German liberties', could hardly seriously envisage a renewal of the Habsburg menace: the looming question

---

[1] E.g. in 1682, when Sweden's military position was too weak for the risk to be taken: Rosén, *Det karolinska skedet*, p. 245.

[2] Nils Bielke in the nineties was intriguing in favour of such a policy, but Bengt Oxenstierna was too strong for him: Carlson, *Sveriges historia*, v, p. 53.

[3] *RRP* III Series, i.i, *Stenografiska Protokoll*, p. 299.

[4] See M. Roberts, 'Cromwell and the Baltic', in Roberts, *Essays in Swedish History* (London 1967), pp. 160ff.

of the Spanish Succession, the threat of the Turk, the problem of Hungary, were more than enough to occupy the none-too-capacious mind of Leopold I, and it is difficult to share Fahlborg's sympathetic *frissons* at the 'standing threat of Habsburg absolutism and Habsburg imperialism in alliance with a still-active Catholic reaction'.[1] If Protestantism was in danger, if the Baltic littoral was threatened, the threat came not from Habsburg but from France – from France, which had helped to subdue the Protestant bastion at Erfurt, and had concluded with the Duke of Mecklenburg–Schwerin a treaty which gave Louis XIV (at least potentially) a naval base in the Baltic.[2] Thus whatever the importance of Pomerania to Sweden's status as a great power, the object for which it had been acquired was no longer relevant: the Pomeranian bastion was the costly relic of a vanished age.

By 1660 one area, and one only, still had real strategic and political significance: the Baltic provinces. The need to maintain the position won at Stolbova had been vividly demonstrated in the 1650s: once Alexis had finally mastered the threat of Tatar invasions, Russia resumed her old thrust to the Baltic. Ordyn-Nashchokin looks back to Ivan IV, and is the presage of Peter. Every consideration – strategic, political, even commercial – must enjoin Swedish statesmen to maintain the land-bridge between Ingria and Finland and oppose an adamantine resistance to the danger that Russia might one day become a naval power.

Apart altogether from these particular cases, it seems clear that the European standing which Sweden acquired at Westphalia was a delusive and wasting asset. Membership of the *Reich* involved the country in policies and disputes of only marginal relevance: in the tedious struggle at Regensburg for a *Reichsverfassung*; in the championship of the cause of the princes against the Electors; in resistance to attempts to subject Münster, or Hildesheim, to Catholic overlords; in the *Wildfangstreit*; in the perennial in-fighting of the three Circles of which Charles XI found himself a member. It is true, no doubt, that the inclusion of Sweden's

[1] Birger Fahlborg, 'Sverige på fredskongressen i Nijmegen, 1676–78', *HT* 1944, pp. 231–2. Nevertheless, the fear persisted, even as late as 1690: see Åke Stille, 'Bengt Oxenstiernas memorial våren 1690', in *Historiska studier tillägnade Nils Ahnlund* (Stockholm 1949), p. 208.

[2] Fahlborg, *Sveriges yttre politik 1660–1664*, p. 450; id., *Sveriges yttre politik 1664–1668*, I, pp. 154ff, 266.

German territories in the League of the Rhine gave Bremen–
Verden immunity from invasion in 1659;[1] but it was not often
that participation in the particularist policies of members of the
Reich brought Sweden any advantage. Far more serious than these
petty concerns were the consequences of Sweden's position as
co-guarantor of the Westphalian settlement. For that dangerous
eminence imposed an obligation to see that the terms of peace,
and the balance which it was supposed to have secured, were
properly observed – an obligation which might mean military
intervention where common-sense would have enjoined absten-
tion; and above all it confronted Sweden repeatedly with the need
to take a position in regard to clashing interpretations of articles
in the peace-treaties which had been left deliberately obscure.
Pre-eminent among these was the notorious clause *Ut eo sincerior*,
which had been designed (perhaps!) to neutralize the Burgundian
Circle. The agonizing dilemmas of the statesmen of the sixties,
wavering between the Habsburg and Bourbon interpretations of
this clause, led at last to the disasters of the seventies. It may be
that Sweden's diplomatic and financial position was such that she
would in any case have ended up in the same predicament; but
it is difficult to avoid the feeling that Magnus Gabriel de la Gardie
and his colleagues must have cursed the fatal ingenuity of Johan
Adler Salvius, who had been responsible for drafting this particular
clause.

How well, then, were the Regents for Charles XI equipped to
face the enlarged responsibilities and increased dangers which
Axel Oxenstierna and Charles X had bequeathed to them?
Sweden had proved capable of creating an empire. Was she also
capable of retaining it?

One of the fundamental facts about the empire was that it was
a naval empire; bound together, but also sundered, by the sea;
dependent upon command of the Baltic for its survival. Swedish
statesmen, from Axel Oxenstierna onwards, realized this perfectly
well,[2] and the maintenance of a strong navy, capable of dealing

---

[1] See Edvard Ehrensteen's *Relation* (1660), in *SRARP* VII.180.

[2] See, e.g., *AOSB* I.vi.37 (to Gustav Adolf, 8 January 1631); *AOSB* I.viii.89 (to
Klas Fleming, 22 January 1633); and his remark in 1636, 'If our fleet has the upper
hand, then we are masters of the Baltic', quoted in N. Ahnlund, *Tradition och historia*
(Stockholm 1956), p. 129.

with any threat from Denmark, was always near the top of their list of priorities. After the crushing victory of Femern in 1644 Sweden's naval supremacy was for the next decade so secure that Christina did not scruple to sell off warships to Louis XIV, and to private creditors, in order to pay her debts.[1] Nevertheless, for much of the period the naval position was by no means assured, as Sweden was to find between 1654 and 1660.[2] In the first place, the more the empire expanded, the more apparent it became that from the naval point of view Stockholm lay too far to the north: the Danish fleets could put to sea a full month before the ice melted in the Stockholm skerries, and even when the water round Stockholm was ice-free, the navigation through the skerries could be so intricate, in unfavourable wind-conditions, that it might take a fleet nine or ten weeks to reach the open sea. Ships had consequently to be provisioned as though for long cruises, or in the alternative might be forced to return home in mid-cruise.[3] For these reasons Charles XI in 1682 transferred his main naval base to the new town of Karlskrona, where the water was warmer, and whence most corners of the Baltic were within easy reach.[4] In the second place, Sweden's command of the sea – and thus the safety of the empire – depended upon the maintenance of the doctrine of *dominium maris Baltici*: the Admiralty in Stockholm must be able to reckon on having to deal with the Danish fleet, and with no other. Hence the provision of the peace of Roskilde (abrogated by the peace of Copenhagen three years later) forbidding the entry of foreign fleets through the Sound. But in fact, on two crucial occasions – in 1659 and 1676 – the Swedish navy had to cope not only with the Danes but with the Dutch. In 1659 the Swedish fleet was penned up in Landskrona by a Dutch squadron, the Swedish armies isolated on Sjaelland by Dutch command of the sea; in 1676 the combined Danish–Dutch fleet inflicted a shattering defeat which cost Sweden three-quarters of

---

[1] For Femern, see Nils F. Holm (ed.), *Det svenska svärdet. Tolv avgörande händelser i Sveriges historia* Stockholm 1948), pp. 148–57; for the naval position thereafter, Försvarsstaben, *Från Femern och Jankow till Westfaliska freden*, pp. 47–50.

[2] See Askgaard, *Kampen om Östersjön, passim*; and cf. Christer Bonde's warning in December 1654: *RRP* xvi.18.

[3] *SRARP* xvi.322–3.

[4] Gustaf Clemensson, *Flottans förläggning till Karlskrona. En studie i flottstationsfrågan före år 1685* Stockholm 1938).

THE UNMAKING OF THE EMPIRE

her capital ships, and which had as its immediate consequence the total loss of Pomerania. Charles XI, whose first preoccupation after 1679 was to rebuild the navy, drew the appropriate inference, and the consequence was the Dutch alliance of 1681. It entailed the sacrifice of long-held Swedish commercial ambitions; but it was a sacrifice which had to be made. For if Sweden was willing to make it, and if she took care not to drift into enmity to the Dutch, she could be sure that Denmark would not be permitted to reverse the verdict of 1660: only under great provocation would the Dutch be prepared to see both shores of the Sound once again in the same hands. After 1683 it became increasingly clear that Sweden would be dependent upon the goodwill of the Maritime Powers for the maintenance of her naval ascendancy in the Baltic. As long as England and Holland were rivals, Denmark might hope to find in one or the other a naval ally and paymaster: in the years after 1666, for instance, the Danish Admiralty was able to launch a massive building programme with the aid of Dutch subsidies.[1] In this situation, the efforts of the Regents in the sixties, and of Charles XI in the early eighties, to give Sweden a strong navy, could never provide full security. That security was not attainable until the English Revolution had put an end to Anglo-Dutch hostility, and so removed one of the chronic dilemmas of both the Scandinavian powers.[2] The Congress of Altona demonstrated the usefulness to Sweden of Anglo-Dutch friendship; the peace of Travendal revealed that that usefulness had its limitations. The command of the sea which Charles XII inherited was subject to the proviso that he did not use it in ways unacceptable to the merchants of London and Amsterdam; and that was a proviso which he was unwise enough to ignore.

If then Sweden could not by her own exertions be sure of keeping her naval supremacy, neither was she able without assistance to defend the empire on land. In quiet times the native army, as established by the Form of Government, might suffice to protect Sweden proper; and the mercenary armies in the

---

[1] Fahlborg, *Sveriges yttre politik 1664–1668*, I, p. 396.
[2] Contrast Fahlborg's view that the union of England and Holland undermined Bengt Oxenstierna's policy, and pushed Sweden towards 'a no-man's land, where political isolation threatened': 'Det senare 1600-talets svenska utrikespolitik', *HT* 1954, p. 107.

provinces, it might be hoped, would safeguard their frontiers from casual raids. But if a serious international crisis threatened these forces were not sufficient: they had to be supplemented by a swift recruitment of mercenaries on a large scale. This might in fact be no more than a strictly precautionary measure which no responsible statesman could avoid in the context of the times: it might imply no aggressive design whatever. But the financial implications were so onerous that they could be borne only if, in the old style of the Thirty Years War, the new levies were transferred to foreign soil with the least possible delay. This was not, of course, a dilemma which was peculiar to Sweden: on the contrary, it was one which also affected Sweden's enemies. The Danish decision to attack in 1657 was in the last resort determined by just such a consideration; and Frederick III pushed his Council into agreeing to it by precisely the same arguments as Charles X had used in 1654 and 1655.[1] Forty years later, it was the fact that after the peace of Karlowitz Augustus II had no other means of keeping his army together which was one main reason for his invasion of Livonia.[2] Nevertheless it remains true that until Charles XI's reforms mobilization for Sweden inevitably led to war; a purely precautionary measure was by a fatal logic translated into an act of aggression.[3] For only by aggression could it be paid for. It proved so in 1654; it was to prove so again in 1675, when the forces in Pomerania which had been designed only as a demonstration to lend weight to diplomatic action were constrained in order to sustain themselves to cross the border into Brandenburg and take the road that was to lead to Fehrbellin.[4] If that road should end in defeat, if a continuation of offensive action thereby became impossible, the prospects were bleak indeed: when in August 1675 Magnus Gabriel de la Gardie told his colleagues that this was in fact the situation, Bengt Horn and Knut Kurck cried out together 'God help us, then; for our

---

[1] Askgaard, *Kampen om Östersjön*, pp. 103–5.

[2] Hjärne, *Karl XII*, p. 61.

[3] As Jens Juel, the Danish ambassador, clearly saw: on 11 July 1674 he wrote to his master, Frederick III 'Once they are strongly armed, they are no longer masters of themselves': A. Fryxell, *Handlingar rörande Sveriges historia, ur utrikes arkiver samlade och utgifne* (Stockholm 1836), I, p. 288.

[4] N. Wimarsson, 'Karl Gustaf Wrangel och brytningen med Brandenburg 1674', *HT* 1920, pp. 24–33.

situation is absolutely desperate!'[1] The empire, it seemed, could be safeguarded only by the application of the same means by which it had been acquired – that is, by maintaining a continuous momentum of expansion. And if expansion should happen to be successful, the dilemma which had made it necessary would recur with increased poignancy after every leap forward.

Once Charles X was dead this was felt to be no longer an acceptable conclusion. For the first time for sixty years Sweden was at peace; and the whole country was determined if possible to remain so. The Regents and the Council were well aware of this feeling, and most of them shared it: old soldiers such as Königsmarck and Wrangel, who urged that for the sake of keeping the army in good trim some little war must be arranged for them somewhere – in Russia, perhaps? – found that their arguments as a rule fell on deaf ears: the fiasco of the Bremen campaign, when for once they had their way, was not an encouraging precedent. Under the leadership of Gustav Bonde the Regents in the early sixties nerved themselves to pursue a policy of stringent economy and the preservation of peace. Almost their first measure was to cut down the size of the army by half. The desperate financial expedients which reduced the debt which Charles X had left behind him undoubtedly impaired the country's ability to wage a war, as Wrangel said that they would: in 1660 the guns of the fleet had to be pawned to pay the shipwrights' wages, and old Per Brahe stated flatly that 'to wage war with Sweden's resources is an *impossibility*'.[2] In 1669 Gustav Kurck was saying that since the peace more men had died of starvation in the mercenary regiments than had been lost in half the campaigns in Poland.[3] In 1671 the Council agreed that it was impossible to maintain an army on German soil adequate to defend Pomerania: Magnus Gabriel de la Gardie said it was 'a dream'.[4] Two years later, when the great European crisis was already upon them, work in the dockyards was at a standstill for lack of money, the troops in Bremen were four years behind with their pay, and a member of the Council could express his opinion that 'there is

---

[1] *RRP* III Series, i.1 *Stenografiska Protokoll*, p. 273.
[2] Fahlborg, *Sveriges yttre politik 1660–1664*, p. 132; Carlson, *Sveriges historia*, II, pp. 26–7, 27 *n*.   [3] Wittrock, *Karl XI:s förmyndares finanspolitik*, II, p. 182.
[4] Birger Fahlborg, 'Sveriges förbund med Frankrike 1672', *HT* 1935, p. 310.

practically no part of our arrangements which is in so pitiable a condition as our army'.[1] It is not perhaps surprising that Feuquières could report that there were some of the Swedish nobility who would not be sorry to lose the German provinces, as being a burden impossible to support.[2] The Baltic provinces, devastated by the catastrophes of the fifties, lay open to invasion. And Gustav Bonde's attempt to put the finances on a sound footing had been irrevocably wrecked by the unsuccessful attack upon Bremen – a typical example of Sweden's inability to shoulder the burden of a military demonstration undertaken for essentially diplomatic objects. Nor had the situation been improved by the wastefulness, incompetence, self-indulgence and sanguine irresponsibility of the Regents themselves.

Yet the alarming fact remained that if any great European conflict should arise Sweden might find it necessary to arm for her own security, and for the security of her German lands. But there could now be no question of recurring to the old solution of extricating themselves from their military–financial problems by means of a war of aggression: the necessary military potential was lacking, and they had no means of their own to supply the indispensable capital, in men and money, without which that solution could not be essayed. Some other method must be found, if the *simulacrum* of greatness was to be maintained, and the safety of the country to be ensured. The only solution that offered was to fish for subsidies, baiting the hook with promises which they hoped to be able to evade, and arguments which wore increasingly thin. De la Gardie might protest that a foreign subsidy was 'an *accessorium* and not *principale*',[3] but if so it was an accessory which the Regents found increasingly difficult to do without. Their hope

[1] Carlson, *Sveriges historia*, II, pp. 293–5. (But see Wittrock, *Karl XI:s förmyndares finanspolitik*, II, pp. 379, 399, for a less unfavourable view of the financial situation.) *RRP* III Series, i.1 *Stenografiska Protokoll 1674–75*, *passim*, for the dilatory incompetence of naval administration, and the Admiralty's feud with the Treasury. In November 1675 Admiral Uggla remarked (with much justification) 'We have no need of enemies, for we destroy ourselves': *ibid.*, p. 350.

[2] Quoted in Carlson, *Sveriges historia*, III, pp. 84, 368, 381. It was a view shared by statesmen of outlook as divergent as Per Brahe and Johan Gyllenstierna: Fahlborg, *Sveriges yttre politik 1664–1668*, I, p. 231; Sven Ulric Palme, 'Sveriges politiska ledning under 1670-talets kris', *HT* 1937, p. 94; G. Landberg, *Johan Gyllenstiernas nordiska förbundspolitik* (Uppsala 1931), p. 100.

[3] Fahlborg, *Sveriges yttre politik 1660–1664*, p. 545. Axel Oxenstierna had been rather franker: 'Necessity is a great argument, and for a handful of gold one must often sacrifice reputation': *RRP* VIII.329 (21 November 1640).

was, that with such financial aid they might be able to put their armed forces on a footing to compel respect for Sweden's neutrality. And if that could be done they believed that it might be possible to hold the balance in the great contentions of the time – the struggles of Bourbon and Habsburg, England and the Dutch – and that the absence of military glory might be compensated by the prestige of acting as mediator.

But the very fact that subsidies were required to make neutrality credible destroyed the basis of this calculation; since no subsidy-granting power was likely for long to accept neutrality as a satisfactory *quid pro quo*. The Regents did not see it. The heirs of Gustav Adolf and Charles X thought so well of their weight in the world that they permitted themselves to believe that any power – ally or enemy – could be persuaded to give them money. To their ally they would argue that merely by arming they had rendered as effective a service as if they had begun hostilities; while they did not blush at the same time to cadge subsidies from their nominal enemy on the ground that they had earned them by keeping the peace. In short, they aspired to welsh both sides simultaneously: an unusual, not to say optimistic, programme.[1] But sooner or later a subsidizing power was going to demand a better bargain than this; sooner or later Sweden would find that the subsidy she had pocketed in order to stay neutral would be used as a lever to force her into war. This happened in 1674, when the French, having paid for Sweden's arming, refused to pay any more until that army was used; with the predictable result that an attack on Brandenburg became unavoidable, in order to save the troops from starvation. Thus the subsidy-system in the end ruined the quite sensible policy of neutrality, balance and mediation which had been its original purpose; and not all Birger Fahlborg's sympathetic exposition of the cruel dilemmas confronting the Regents can really disguise their fatal lack of realism and statesmanlike insight.[2]

[1] See, e.g., typical instances of this naive deviousness in Fahlborg, *Sveriges yttre politik 1660–1664*, p. 409, and *id.*, *Sveriges yttre politik 1664–1668*, I, p. 381; or the remarks of Nils Brahe, quoted in Carlson, *Sveriges historia*, II, p. 181; or the desperate debate in the Council on 16 September 1674: *RRP* III Series, i.1 *Stenografiska Protokoll 1674–75*, especially pp. 50–1.

[2] In May 1673 de la Gardie advised his colleagues to 'do as France did in the late king's time, and form a Hague Concert': Carlson, *Sveriges historia*, II, pp. 308–9. Apparently he did not grasp that Hague Concerts were only likely to be successful if

Small wonder if Sweden's reputation sank rapidly in the twenty years after 1660, and that foreign statesmen very soon responded to her leaders' inflated ideas of their country's importance with something which began as scepticism and ended as contempt. Sweden had lost that invaluable diplomatic asset, reputation; and de la Gardie and his colleagues in time were driven to face that bitter truth.[1] They tried in vain to conceal it by dispendious embassies, paid for sometimes with subsidy-money which would have been better employed on the military purposes for which it had been given,[2] and almost always disproportionate to the results achieved and to the resources available. At home, it was as though men sought, by ostentatious adoption of the trappings and standards of a great power, to persuade themselves that they were still the nation that had won the Thirty Years War. Never had national pride been higher, nor the overt manifestations of patriotism more strident, than in the age which produced Pufendorf's *History of the Deeds of Charles X*, Olof Rudbeck's *Atlantica*, and that splendid propaganda-exercise, Erik Dahlberg's *Suecia Antiqua et Hodierna*. The old austerity of Swedish life and manners is replaced by that bloated Baroque, that lush luxuriousness in dress, living-standards, art and architecture, which impressed the foreign visitor, and made Stockholm one of the most expensive capitals of Europe for a diplomat to live in: the Sweden which Magalotti saw in 1672 would have seemed unrecognizable to Charles Ogier, who visited it forty years earlier. The arts and learning flourished under de la Gardie's generous and discriminating patronage: if his income was preposterously large,[3] at least he spent a good deal of it in ways

they had teeth in them. Bengt Oxenstierna, who likewise hankered for a Hague Concert in 1690, realized that even then it would require more troops in Germany than Sweden could afford, to make it credible: Stille, 'Bengt Oxenstiernas memorial våren 1690', p. 211.

[1] On 20 September 1669 de la Gardie wrote to Edvard Ehrensteen: 'My heart breaks to see with what indignity all this time Sweden is now treated, and that such a glorious crown is losing its reputation more and more': *Historiska handlingar*, VIII, p. 81. And *cf.* Carlson, *Sveriges historia*, III, pp. 11–12 n; Fahlborg, *Sveriges yttre politik 1664–1668*, I, pp. 479, 491.

[2] Wittrock, *Karl XI:s förmyndares finanspolitik*, I, p. 248; Fahlborg, 'Sveriges förbund med Frankrike 1672', p. 317.

[3] About 310,000 silver *dalers*, or roughly £85,000 at contemporary rates of exchange: Göran Landahl, *Magnus Gabriel de la Gardie. Hans gods och hans folk*

which entitle him to the gratitude of posterity. The high nobility were building those splendid palaces which Erik Dahlberg's tactful pencil was to immortalize – and improve. The fashions of Paris were transplanted to the unsuitable climate of Stockholm; orangeries were somehow coaxed into existence; and the youthful Charles XI was made to feature in a pseudo-Roman *caroussel*. But anyone less suited than Charles XI to the attempt to ape Louis XIV it would be difficult to imagine; nor any country which could better have spared such excesses than Sweden. But the Roman helmets, the waving plumes, the gilt armour, the caparisoned chargers, did something to offset the growing feeling that Sweden had somehow got politically out of her depth. And if the Council of State, torn by feuds and factions, and groping for some way out of the labyrinths in which it found itself, chose this moment to introduce those splendid senatorial robes of ermine and purple which were to be its badge of office for long afterwards, this too may perhaps be seen as an unconscious effort to stiffen morale.[1]

Between 1675 and 1679 the political system of the Regents, at home and abroad, sustained blows from which it could never recover. The policy of neutrality and balance had brought an unwanted and ruinous war; the navy had been all but annihilated; Pomerania was lost, Livonia defenceless, Skåne in full revolt in support of Denmark; and the financial situation was desperate. Charles XI's blind valour at the battle of Lund had indeed saved his country from outright defeat at Denmark's hands; but only the imperious intervention of Louis XIV had availed to restore Sweden to the *status quo ante bellum*. It might seem that this was the end of Sweden's greatness: in the eyes of Europe she now appeared as no more than the client and *protégé* of France. The saga had closed, not only in defeat, but in humiliation.

But, against all expectations, there followed a great recovery.

(Stockholm 1968), p. 33. For Claes Tott's censure of contemporary ostentatious expenditure, see Carlson, *Sveriges historia*, III, p. 312 *n*; for the last fling of the high aristocracy before the deluge, see Jens Juel's account of Magnus de la Gardie's great feast for Charles XI in May 1680: Fryxell, *Handlingar rörande Sveriges historia*, I, p. 386. The change after 1679 is perhaps illustrated by the reduced scale of noble funerals thereafter: see *Landshöfdingen Friherre Gabriel Kurcks lefnadsminnen* (Helsingfors 1906), pp. 174–6, 195 (though admittedly on the first of these two occasions he was burying his wife, on the second, his sister-in-law).

[1] First used at Charles XI's coronation in 1675: Carlson, *Sveriges historia*, II, p. 351.

Defeat and humiliation, by a not unfamiliar alchemy, produced a medicine, and perhaps a cure, for the ills which had baffled the Regents. The specific was indeed drastic; but at least it seemed effective. It consisted, of course, in the establishment of a popular absolutism. The change was made possible by the personal prestige of the monarch as the saviour of his country, by the hostility of the three lower Estates to the Estate of Nobility, by the desperate need of civil servants to see the crown in a position to pay them their wages, and by the antagonism of the lesser nobility to the great magnates of the Council. It was an absolutism solidly based on parliamentary support; it was strong because it had the backing of the greater part of the nation. No government less powerfully supported could have carried through the reforms which Charles XI imposed upon Sweden in the decade after 1680. No solution to the problem of the empire's survival was really conceivable without the radically new approach which those reforms implied. The absolutism presented Sweden with a way out of her dilemma, and that way probably offered the empire its last chance.

Since the death of Charles X, the central problem of government had been that it had seemed impossible for Sweden from her own resources to support an army and navy strong enough to safeguard herself and her provinces, much less to discharge her obligations as guarantor of Westphalia. It was above all to the solution of this problem that Charles XI's efforts were directed. The *reduktion*, and the retributive inquisition into the Regents and the Council, had of course obvious social implications: they smashed the high nobility; they probably saved the peasantry from a progressive deterioration of their social and economic status and from the erosion of their constitutional rights; they strengthened the monarchy not only economically but by disabling the class which was most likely, and best able, to set limits to the power of the crown. But their essential purpose was military: the massive increases in revenue which they were designed to furnish were from the beginning earmarked for spending on defence – upon the navy first of all, and then upon fortifications. The *reduktion* was also used to provide a new basis for the support of the army. Instead of the old conscription, each

province now contracted to supply a fixed quota of men; and by
the so-called 'allocation system' (*indelningsverket*) the farms which
had been resumed into the king's hands were each to house, feed
and equip a soldier, receiving in return his labour services in
peace-time.[1] The effect was to provide the country with a new
territorial army, but at the same time to take the burden of
supporting it from the state's shoulders. It was crucial to the
success of the scheme that these farmer-soldiers should receive
proper training in peacetime; and it became Charles XI's especial
care to see that this happened. Men from different districts were
called up in rotation for shorter or longer periods of training, and
that training was highly effective. The result of these reforms was
that when Charles XI died in 1697 Sweden found herself with a
well-armed, highly-trained army of 90,000 men, instantly available at call, with its concentration-points, its march-routes, its
halts on the road to its destination, all carefully laid down and
provided for. The new army was matched by the new navy,
which by 1697 numbered 34 ships of the line and 11 frigates.[2]
Charles XII inherited from his father the finest army and the
strongest navy that Sweden had ever hitherto possessed. No doubt
it is true that the size of the army seemed now to be fixed by the
number of farms allocated for its maintenance; but the event was
to show that an absolute sovereign would find means easily
enough to overstep that limit. And though it might be a question
whether the army was big enough for offensive warfare, contemporaries were probably right to consider that it was fully
adequate for defence.[3]

There remained, however, the question whether even yet the
state could stand the large expenditures associated with the initial
phases of any war: the provision, for instance, of food and fodder
for the army once it was mobilized, the purchase of extraordinary
supplies of powder and armaments, the cost of commissioning and

[1] Sven Ågren, *Karl XI:s indelningsverk för armén. Bidrag till dess historia åren 1679–1697*
(Uppsala 1922), *passim*.
[2] Rosén, *Det karolinska skedet*, p. 277. An Italian visitor in 1696 observed 'Though
the country was at peace, it gave the impression of being mobilized for war': E. Tegnér,
Svenska bilder från sextonhundratalet (Stockholm 1896), p. 264.
[3] Hans Landberg, 'Kungamaktens emancipation. Statsreglering och militärorgan-
isation under Karl X Gustav och Karl XI', *Scandia* 1969, p. 127.

provisioning the navy, the cost of hiring transports. This was the difficulty that had driven Charles X to all sorts of emergency measures; this had been a main reason for the Regents' acceptance of French subsidies in 1672. But Charles XI had foreseen the difficulty and made provision for it: a great hoard of treasure in the vaults of Stockholm castle, a half-dozen or so of fat reserve funds which could be raided in an emergency. And despite the fact that between 1697 and 1700 these assets were to an alarming extent dissipated by purely civil expenditures,[1] when the crisis came in 1700 they proved sufficient to meet it. Eli Heckscher long ago put forward the view that Charles XI's reforms must bear some responsibility for the collapse of the Swedish empire: they reduced liquidity, substituted revenues in kind for revenues in cash, destroyed the crown's credit and clamped the country's civil and military organization into rigid patterns which could not be adapted to the stress of war. The hoarding of treasure, like the reversion to revenues in kind, excited his derision as an economist; and he did not hesitate to write of the 'idea-less' Charles XI.[2] But the researches of Dr Cavallie have modified these ideas and done much to refute Heckscher's objections.[3] The machine *did* prove adaptable; the hoards were a wise precaution precisely because Charles XI realized that the crown's credit was poor; and, after all, two-thirds of the state's revenues were still in cash, and readily available. Charles XI had more ideas, and a much more realistic appreciation of the situation, than Heckscher gave him credit for. He left behind him an army and navy, a financial system, well able to sustain the immediate impact of war. Moreover, in 1700, when Charles XII virtually suspended the operations of the *reduktion* and the inquisition, the problem of internal credit vanished too: between 1701 and 1708 deposits in the Bank went up by 143%, and it was able to lend the crown something like

---

[1] Including the redemption of the small German territory of Wildeshausen, which had been pawned to the Bishop of Münster by Charles XI – a striking example of the excessive preoccupation with Germany. A few years later Charles XII had to pawn it again: Cavallie, *Från fred till krig*, p. 47.

[2] Heckscher, *Sveriges ekonomiska historia* I, pp. 2, 288ff; *id.*, *Ekonomi och historia*, p. 92.

[3] Cavallie, *Från fred till krig*, *passim*; *cf.* Landberg, 'Kungamaktens emancipation', p. 126. For some qualifications of Cavallie's conclusions (which, however, do not seem to me to impair them seriously) see Roland Persson, *Rustningar i Sverige under det stora nordiska kriget* (Lund 1975).

six millions.[1] In 1700, it is clear, Sweden was better equipped to wage war than ever before.

Thus after 1680 Charles XI and his advisers created a military system which provided secure defence, and an economic basis for that system which made the ignominious hunt for foreign subsidies unnecessary. The success of the endeavour was reflected in a firmer and more self-reliant foreign policy. The aims of that policy were neutrality, the European balance, perhaps a 'Third Party', above all, peace: the same programme, in fact, as that of the Regents; but a programme now made credible by Sweden's new-found military and financial independence.[2] Charles could now afford to snub the French ambassador and break off diplomatic relations with Louis XIV;[3] he could risk participation in an armed neutrality designed to curb the privateering excesses of the Maritime Powers. He was even willing to fight, if no other resort seemed possible, to save Holstein–Gottorp from Denmark. But on the whole he made prudence his watchword, asking nothing better than to be left alone: 'a war is soon begun', he wrote, 'but its outcome lies in God's hands'[4] – and on those terms he preferred not to risk it. It was a conscious evasion of dangerous international obligations, a clear-eyed recognition of the limits of his country's capacity to act. The historic attempt to seek a solution to Sweden's problems by expansion, by 'aggression', was tacitly abandoned, apparently for ever. The Lion of the North had been transmogrified into a hedgehog.

The main danger, in the eighties, seemed to come from Denmark; and Charles could never forget how near Denmark had come to success in 1676. Throughout the eighties Denmark steadily pursued the design of absorbing Holstein–Gottorp, and thus removing the Swedish threat to her back door. In 1683 only the veto of Louis XIV prevented the conquest by Denmark and

[1] C. L. Lundquist, *King and Estates in Sweden 1713–1714* (Stockholm 1975), p. 95; Ulf Brandell, 'Förändringen i den svenska statshushållningen under det stora nordiska kriget', KFÅ 1941, pp. 77–80.
[2] See Åke Stille, *Studier över Bengt Oxenstiernas politiska system och Sveriges förbindelser med Danmark och Holstein–Gottorp 1689–92* (Uppsala 1947); and Gustaf Jonasson, *Karl XII och hans rådgivare. Den utrikespolitiska maktkampen 1697–1702* (Uppsala 1960), pp. 278–80.
[3] Carlson, *Sveriges historia*, III, p. 326; IV, p. 113.
[4] *Karl XI:s bref till Nils Bielke* (*Historiska Handlingar* XVIII, no. 2) (Stockholm 1900), p. 48.

Brandenburg of Sweden's German possessions; but even so a French fleet in the Sound threatened a Franco-Danish attack on Charles XI's new navy, and from this imminent peril it appeared to have been delivered only by the appearance (albeit belated) of a Dutch squadron.[1] It was no wonder that Bengt Oxenstierna held his master firmly to the alliance with the Maritime Powers, whose navies alone could give Sweden the assurance she needed. No wonder either that the money lavished on fortifications went in the main into safeguarding the country from another Danish invasion. Yet however intelligible, the fear of Denmark was a miscalculation. After 1680 the international situation was such that Christian V could not really hope to subject Holstein–Gottorp, and still less to recover Halland and Skåne. The real threat to Sweden came, not from Denmark, but from Russia. It is hardly surprising that statesmen in Stockholm thought otherwise. If ever there was a period when the danger from Russia might seem to be less imminent, it was in the decade or so that followed the death of Alexis: a period when Russia was weakened first by palace revolutions, and then deeply committed to the war against the Turks.[2] But, however hard to recognize, the danger was there. It had always been there, from Sten Sture's time onwards. Even the pacific Gustav Vasa had felt bound to meet it in arms. It had been the danger from the east that had first impelled Sweden to a career of overseas expansion. Gustav Adolf had erected a barrier against it. Charles X had identified it as the greatest threat his country had to fear. The Regents had felt it looming over them, and more than once had half-heartedly debated a preventive war, as the best hope of keeping it at a distance.[3] Charles XII would at last succumb to it. But Charles XI's foreign policy, designed to give him security in the south and west, left him naked and friendless in the east.[4] His military measures left too many troops

---

[1] For the crisis see A. Lossky, *Louis XIV, William III, and the Baltic crisis of 1683* (Berkeley 1954).

[2] See Klaus Zernack, *Studien zu den schwedisch-russischen Beziehungen in den 2. Hälfte des 17. Jahrhunderts*, I (Giessen 1958).

[3] Fahlborg, *Sveriges yttre politik 1660–1664*, pp. 311–12; Wittrock, *Karl XI:s förmyndares finanspolitik*, II, pp. 264, 315.

[4] As Georg Landberg remarked, 'Sweden's policy as a great power in the last resort must be one and indivisible' – in the east no less than in the west: Landberg, 'Sveriges yttre politik, 1660–1668', *HT* 1950, p. 219.

in Germany, too few in Estonia;[1] his concentration on defensive works against Denmark meant that fortifications in the Baltic lands were ruinous or non-existent – as they had been, indeed, for the last two generations.[2] Charles XI was not unaware of the danger: Erik Dahlberg and others sent him explicit and reiterated warnings. And in the end, a little was done. But in this respect, as in some others, Charles lacked that precious commodity – time.

The miscalculation was certainly serious. But it was not fatal. The empire was not lost because Erik Dahlberg's remonstrances for long went unheeded. In 1700 Charles XI's system was subjected to strains far exceeding the worst that its creators can ever have envisaged: simultaneous attacks, unprovoked, almost unheralded, from Denmark, Saxony and Russia. And it stood the test, militarily and politically. The alliance with the Maritime Powers made it possible to knock out Denmark before the danger in the east grew uncontrollable. The defences of the Baltic provinces somehow held fast; the king's assault crushed the Russians at Narva; Stuart's experience and Swedish valour forced the Düna, defeated Augustus, and put Kurland in Charles's possession.

Sweden's military commitments were now limited to a single theatre of war; and it is not easy to believe that in these circumstances its defence was not well within the power of the forces upon which Charles XII was able to draw. It is often argued, not without some force, that Sweden's military successes had depended, and would continue to depend, upon the use of her transmarine bridgeheads for offensive, and not for defensive, operations; that, in the words of Professor Lundkvist, 'A defensive strategy, based on the home country and the provinces, was

---

[1] In 1700 there were 10,150 mercenary troops in Germany, as against 6,700 in the Baltic provinces: Cavallie, *Från fred till krig*, p. 35; but in 1699 there had been no more than 1,400 in Livonia, *plus* a garrison of 2,000 in Riga: Dunsdorfs, *Der grosse schwedische Kataster*, p. 187.

[2] Some fortresses – e.g. Jama – had passed from the crown into private hands, and been allowed to become ruinous: *SRARP* v₂.70 (1655). Contrast the official optimism about the state of the fortifications in *SRARP* xv.390–1 (1689) and *ibid.* xvi.92 (1693), with the more sober report in *ibid.* xvi.339 (1697). In that year 213,000 *d.s.m.* was allotted to work on defences against Denmark, as against 177,674 on defences in the Baltic provinces: *Dela Gardieska Archivet* xii, pp. 34–5. And see, e.g., *AOSB* ii.x.344 (1633); Carlson, *Sveriges historia*, i, p. 297 (1656); Fahlborg, *Sveriges yttre politik 1664–1668*, i, pp. 59, 308, 538 (1665–6).

simply not practicable, since in the long run they lacked the resources to produce the dynamic thrust that was required.'[1] But this is an argument which begs the question whether a 'dynamic thrust' still *was* required. Charles XI clearly had not thought so. It was no longer true to say of Sweden, '*vivitur ex rapto*'. The military and financial reforms of the eighties and nineties had, after all, been designed for purposes of defence: the armies which Charles XI left behind him, as Gustaf Jonasson put it, were

never intended to be led to Dresden, Kraków and Pultava. If Charles XII had used his father's military apparatus in accordance with his intentions, it is perhaps not entirely impossible that Sweden's position as a great state might have been granted a somewhat longer span of life.[2]

The crucial question, however, was whether armies adequate to the task of defence could be maintained and supplied from the resources available on the spot, and from stores to be ferried over from their Swedish base.[3] It might seem that Sweden was once again confronted with the familiar dilemma: either she must impose crushing burdens on her own territories, or she must somehow contrive to shift them to the shoulders of her enemies. But in 1701 the situation in these respects was far less desperate than it had been (for instance) in 1636. And yet at that time Pomerania had somehow been held. A solution of the dilemma might very well have lain in an occupation of Russian territory as far as (say) Ladoga, Pskov and Gdov: this was the plan advocated by Stuart before the crossing of the Düna;[4] it was the

[1] Lundkvist, 'An Experience of Empire', pp. 28, 38–9.
[2] Gustaf Jonasson, reviewing Cavallie, *Från fred till krig*, in *HT* 1975, p. 492.
[3] For some doubts on this see Åke Stille, 'Några synpunkter på den svenska krigsmaktens historia med särskild hänsyn till sjövapnets roll', *Skrifter utg. av Sjöhistoriska Samfundet* 1941.
[4] For a discussion of the implication of Stuart's plan, and the reason for its abandonment, see Göran Rystad, 'Ryssland eller Polen? Karl XII:s planer efter Dünaövergången. Några synpunkter', *Scandia* 1961. From a review by David Kirby of O. Korkiakangas: *Kaarle XII:n kenttäarmeijan huolto sotarekillä vuosina 1700–1701 mannereurooppalaisten huoltojärjestelmien näkökulmasta* (Helsinki 1974) in *EHR* xci, 647–8 (1976) it would appear that Korkiakangas argues that by Charles XII's time armies had come to depend increasingly on magazines, which demanded expensive fortifications, and these Sweden could not afford. But in fact large sums were spent on fortifications – in what turned out to be the wrong places. Kirby, apparently summarizing Korkiakangas's argument, contends that Russian devastation in eastern Estonia, and lack of supplies in Kurland, caused Charles's push into Lithuania: 'The Swedish king's

plan which Gustav Adolf had pursued eighty-five years before. It would have protected the Baltic provinces, shifted the burden on to enemy soil, and still left Charles free to defend himself against Augustus. The Baltic provinces had not at this stage been so harried by the Russian armies as to destroy their capacity to serve as a base – either for a purely defensive campaign, or (if that were judged essential) for an offensive towards Moscow. Certainly there seems good reason to suppose that such an offensive, if launched at any time between 1701 and 1703, and based on the Baltic provinces, a short line of communications, and access to the sea, had a better chance of success than the enterprise of 1708–9, based on Poland – or the wasting asset of a mobile base, as provided by Lewenhaupt's army – and dependent on a line of communications of almost impossible length and difficulty.[1]

It is no part of my purpose to wade into the Serbonian bog of controversy as to Charles's plans and his merits as a strategist, though the paucity of hard evidence on the subject offers an agreeable freedom to intelligent speculation. But it would probably be conceded by all parties that he seems to have believed that the danger from Russia could be dealt with only by what is called 'a radical solution'; and many historians, even though not professed disciples of the new school of Caroline historiography (now more than half a century old) have been disposed to agree with him.[2] I confess I do not find this argument persuasive. Gustav Adolf in his day had sought a radical solution in Germany. Charles X had looked for one in Poland, and subsequently in Denmark. Neither had found one; and it was well for Sweden that they did not. In Charles XII's case I doubt if it was attainable. Nor am I convinced that it was necessary – at least, in this war. No doubt

decision to invade Poland was greatly influenced by this specific problem of supply, as the author rightly maintains.' But, as Rystad makes clear, the abandonment of Stuart's plan to turn against Russia was caused essentially by *political* factors.

[1] This was Frederick the Great's opinion: cited in C. von Rosen, *Bidrag till kännedomen om de händelser som närmast föregingo svenska stormaktens fall* (Stockholm 1936), II, p. 2 *n* 28.

[2] E.g. Rosén, *Det karolinska skedet*, p. 338. Professor Hatton writes (*Charles XII of Sweden* (London 1968), p. 249): 'once the army of a country basically poor in manpower had been mobilized and trained in action, the disbanding of it was virtually impossible before a radical solution of the problem which had called it into being was secured'. But the armies of Charles XII were mostly native armies; and it was precisely one of the advantages of *indelningsverket* that it largely obviated the problem of disbandment, at least for the greater part of the army.

Charles XI's essentially static foreign policy could not be in-
definitely prolonged in the face of the strong forces that beat
upon it. Sooner or later Sweden would have had to come to terms
with the fact that there was arising to the east of her a power of
a different order of magnitude, with whose vast human and
material resources she could not hope to compete; and before she
accepted that verdict it was no doubt open to her to seek to abort
the threat by a total military victory. It may be conceded that such
a victory was unlikely to prove permanent. But it was not obvious
in 1701 that the attempt had become necessary: the threat from
Russia had not yet developed so far as to make it so; the Russian
thrust to the sea, checked in Ingria, might well in the sequel have
been diverted to lines which offered less resistance – to Windau,
Libau, and even to Memel, all of which were more easily
controllable by Swedish sea-power than Schlüsselburg and St
Petersburg. A victorious peace which stopped short of annihilation
was certainly conceivable, and probably obtainable.

These, however, are matters of opinion. What is a matter of
fact is that the loss of the Baltic provinces, which began with the
fall of Nöteborg and ended with the fall of Riga in 1710, was a
decisive disaster, which not all Charles's Turkish diplomacy could
ever have retrieved. Had the Turks at the Pruth imposed the terms
which Charles desired, Peter could have been relied upon to act
as Francis I acted after Pavia. It was a disaster strategically, in the
first place. It prised open the hinge of Sweden's position on the
Gulf of Finland; it confronted Sweden with a new and formidable
naval power in the Baltic, in defiance of the historic principle of
dominium maris; it uncovered Finland, Åland, and ultimately
Sweden itself; it destroyed the only portion of the empire which
it was vital to preserve.[1] Some of Charles's servants saw this
clearly: as early as 22 December 1702 Nils Lillieroth wrote to
Count Piper, 'If the Tsar be suffered to organize a navy in the
Baltic, he will become one of the mightiest potentates in the
world.'[2] For a layman, uncommitted to the fierce polemics which
encompass Charles XII, it is difficult to accept, without a silent
pursing of the lips, a strategic appreciation which holds the loss
of Nöteborg to have been of less importance than the capture of

---

[1] See Arnold Munthe, *Karl XII och den ryska sjömakten*, I–III (Stockholm 1924–7).
[2] Cited in Stig Backman's review of Munthe, *Karl XII och den ryska sjömakten*, KFÅ
1927, p. 160.

Kraków.[1] The Baltic provinces after 1701 were for Charles XII
what the Lower Saxon Circle and the Thuringian bottle-neck
were for Gustav Adolf: the vital strategic area which must at all
costs be held. It may be true that in the one case as in the other
the position was endangered by the incompetence or jealousies of
the commanders on the spot; and it is certain that in each the
presence of the king became an urgent necessity. Gustav Adolf
learned the hard lesson that few operations are more counter-
productive than diversions which do not divert; Charles XII
provided a lamentable example of this truth when he attempted
to relieve the pressure on Narva by an expedition against Lwów.
Gustav Adolf in the end squarely confronted the strategic crisis,
and at Lützen, in spite of everything, he surmounted it; but when
the decisive moment came at Erastfehr in 1701, Charles XII was
not merely absent: he was looking the other way. It was also a
disaster politically; for it led almost inevitably to the alienation
of the Maritime Powers, already irritated by Charles's occupation
of Kurland, by his treatment of Danzig, and by his aloofness to
their attempts to involve him in the War of the Spanish
Succession. For the Maritime Powers were as anxious to continue
their trade to Narva and Riga, after those ports had passed into
Russian hands, as Charles now was to intercept it. And the
alienation of the Maritime Powers removed the only effective
safeguard against a stab in the back from Denmark. It was
certainly a disaster economically, for it deprived Sweden of the
very substantial revenues which she had latterly been receiving
from Livonia, and of the large grain shipments which came from
that province:[2] their importance to Sweden can be gauged from
the fact that one of the terms of the peace of Nystad guaranteed
to Sweden the right to purchase grain from Livonia in the future,
to a value of 50,000 roubles in any one year. And not least, it was
a disaster morally. For the Baltic provinces seemed to have been
lost (and I believe that they were lost) by the king's negligence
and indifference.[3] The most important strategic positions in the

[1] *Ibid.*, p. 150.

[2] See Ulf Brandell, 'Förändringen i den svenska statshushållningen', pp. 72–3.

[3] The most damning and detailed account of the combination of negligence and
incompetence which led to the loss of the Baltic provinces is in von Rosen, *Bidrag till
kännedomen*, II, p. 2. Munthe's book (*Karl XII och den ryska sjömakten*) was written under
the influence of the supposed danger to Sweden from Bolshevik Russia: it is polemical
in tone and unnecessarily repetitious, but its central contention is not easy to refute.

empire, the only overseas provinces which still fully answered the purposes for which they had been acquired, were allowed to go by default; and their recovery was made dependent upon a concatenation of circumstances so unlikely that it could be believed in only on the basis of *credo quia impossibile*. It was not Charles XI, as Heckscher seemed to suggest, who was responsible for the loss of the Swedish empire. If we are so unwise as to try to pin that responsibility upon a single scapegoat, Charles XII looks in all respects to be a more eligible candidate.

But to do this, of course, is neither meaningful nor just. Like Gustav Adolf and Charles X, he was confronted – and at a very early age – with a catena of choices; and it can perhaps be said of him, as of them, that at each moment of decision he was driven by a logic, compelling to himself if unintelligible to others, to make the choice he did. Even if he had chosen otherwise, if he had been content (as it was not in his nature to be) with something less than the optimum and the absolute, if he had accepted compromises, husbanded his resources, and retired watchfully behind his defences to devote himself to those works of peace which he was so well fitted to undertake[1] – even then, the tide of events was bearing Sweden inexorably away from the position of moral and military authority which had been hers in 1648. As Axel Oxenstierna had long ago perceived, Sweden had owed her greatness to an exceptional international situation:[2] the temporary weakness of her neighbours, the disarray or preoccupation of states better equipped to shoulder the burdens of greatness. Those burdens had from the beginning been too great for Sweden to bear for long, and she had contrived to bear them only by expedients which in the long run made them even heavier. Charles XI's hedgehog policy might indeed preserve the realm which he had inherited for a couple of generations; but it was in itself the sign that Sweden must henceforward trim her responsibilities to match her resources. And her resources were not the resources of a great power. It was, no doubt, unfortunate that the

---

[1] For Charles XII as a peace-king *manqué* see Ragnhild Hatton, *Charles XII of Sweden* (London 1968), especially pp. 337–50.

[2] Sweden's safety, he remarked, consisted in 'Libertas statuum imperii Germaniae; nimia servitus Moscoviae; Poloniae nimia libertas; Daniae interna mala': *RRP* XII.212 (29 October 1647).

end came as it did: the abdication of greatness, as Charles XI had shown, did not necessarily entail Charles XII's private version of *Götterdämmerung*. But sooner or later, in some form or other, the end was certain. And when it came, the only salve which could be offered to assuage the sting of defeat was that Scandinavian alternative for which Axel Oxenstierna once had hankered, which Charles X had vainly pursued, and which was to be Sweden's dubious *solatium* in 1815.

Thus the question implicitly raised at the beginning of this chapter can now, perhaps, be answered. The empire did not fall because it had outlived the purposes for which it had been created. On the contrary, it fell because precisely those provinces which were still discharging a vital political function were allowed to be overwhelmed. This explanation, if it is accepted, rules out or qualifies certain other explanations which might appear to be available. It was not the case, for instance, that a common concern with the preservation of the Balance of Power was bound sooner or later to provoke a hostile European coalition.[1] That situation had certainly arisen in 1658, when Lisola worked for a European coalition against Sweden, as he was later to work for a European coalition against France; but in 1700 no one could seriously contend that Sweden posed any threat to her neighbours. Again, the admitted economic weakness of the country, though serious, was not immediately fatal: it was not, as Ellen Fries once wrote, 'the real Pultava'.[2] Nor is it true that the empire fell because its strength had been sapped by the luxury and self-indulgence of the ruling classes. The Roman virtues of the generation that made the empire had not been enervated by success: in valour, endurance and military discipline the blue-coats of Klissow and Fraustadt had no need to fear comparison with their grandfathers who fought at Breitenfeld. It was no decadent power that crumbled after Pultava. Already in Charles XI's time the swelling pomp of Swedish baroque, in architecture as in life-style, had been sharply curbed; and in its place had come more severely classical ideas, and a way of life more suited to the Spartan austerity of himself and his son. The Swedes confronted the final act of the drama with tightened belts and few illusions. No doubt absolutism itself, as

[1] As suggested by Backman, *KFÅ* 1927, p. 92.
[2] Ellen Fries, 'Johan Classon Risingh', *HT* 1896, p. 72.

a form of government, must bear a large share of the responsibility: at the end, the silent monarch is surrounded by a great silence, broken only by the groans of a suffering people. Charles XI's new Council falls silent under his successor, as the old had fallen silent after 1682; powerless to halt the progress to disaster, thrust aside by the absolutism's private agents, reduced to waiting (and perhaps to hoping) for the end. No doubt it is true, as the history of our own time amply testifies, that empires can be lost by failure of nerve, national exhaustion, and the erosion of the will to rule. Yet before 1709, at all events, that was not the case with Sweden. The immediate cause of the collapse of the empire was an avoidable military catastrophe. The fundamental causes were such as neither the intrepidity of Charles XII, nor the dogged caution of Charles XI, could ever avail to remove.

It has sometimes been said that Sweden's Age of Greatness was a historical aberration: an aberration which may perhaps have been inescapable, but still an aberration; something out of line with the essential trends of Sweden's development, and in any deeper sense irrelevant to it. This may indeed be the truth; but if so, it is a truth which requires modification. And whether true or not, the Age of Greatness cannot simply be dismissed as an episode of no permanent significance. For it sowed seeds which were to bear rich fruit in the future, and it left traces which are still discernible, memories which still form a part of the Swedish national consciousness. The peace of Nystad, after all, did not wipe the slate clean: Sweden did not return in 1721 to the position in which Eric XIV had found her in 1560. Thanks to Carteret's diplomacy the provinces gained from Denmark were not lost; and they included some of the richest agricultural areas in Scandinavia. The impetus given to economic development by the demands of the great wars did not cease to be operative once they were over, and the immigrant *entrepreneurs* remained to enrich still further a country which they had already learned to call their own. The Age of Greatness reinforced Sweden's human resources: not only in numbers, but in quality, in range, in *expertise*. It left behind it visible memorials on a scale such as the early Vasas had never known: the splendours of Caroline Stockholm, with its array of noble palaces; the great castles and country houses which contrasted so strongly with what Goeteeris had seen a century earlier. Much of this, alas, has since been destroyed by fire, and on the remainder a misplaced conformism has all too often imposed the heavy hand of undistinguished classicism; but Läckö, Skokloster, Tidö, and many more, crammed as they are with the plunder of half Europe, survive as witnesses to Sweden's former greatness.

And the booty, after all, meant much more than those 'trophies' which in the black year 1710 the *riksdag* for a moment thought of putting up for auction, and which now adorn *Livrustkammaren*. It included the libraries of Riga, Braunsberg, Würzburg and Mainz; it brought to Uppsala its greatest bibliographical treasure, Ulfilas' silver Bible. Acquisitions such as these gave a spur to Swedish scholarship, and for the first time afforded an adequate base upon which to develop it. The effect was seen in the decades after 1660, notably in the circle which gathered round (and quarrelled with) Olof Rudbeck. The interests of that universal genius ranged from medicine to bridge-building, from botany to the fantastic speculations of *Atlantica*. The Swedes of the seventeenth century planned their works on a scale which matched the grandeur of their country's political pretensions; their scholarly activities were cast in a colossal mould. Rudbeck, for instance, not content with the gigantic cloud-castle of *Atlantica*, could embark with superb confidence, single-handed, upon a compendium which was to describe and illustrate every plant in the known world. Much of what they did has an interest only for those who wander in the by-ways and dead-ends of the history of learning; but much too was subsumed into the more scientific labours of the generation that came after them. Without the characteristic spirit, and the no less characteristic endurance, of the men of the Age of Greatness, the brilliance of the scientific achievements of the Age of Liberty would scarcely have been possible: Linnaeus, Celsius, Bergman, Scheele, struck root in a soil which had been prepared and composted by the experience of empire. So too the new historiography of the eighteenth century, which may be said to have its real beginnings with Dalin and LagerBring, rested in great measure upon the collections of sources undertaken by such men as Messenius, Hadorph, Schmedeman and Peringskiöld. And without the economic advance which the wars had accelerated Sweden might have had to wait longer for a Polhem and a Triewald.

Defeat, disaster, the loss of greatness: these are experiences whose effect upon the societies which undergo them has proved to be neither uniform nor predictable. In Sweden the loss of empire was not for many years accepted as a final verdict. Three times in the course of the eighteenth century attempts were made to upset it; and as late as 1845 there were those who believed that the future Charles XV was destined once more to plant the Swedish flag upon the ramparts of St Petersburg.[1] Swedish foreign policy in the Age of Freedom, whichever party might be in power, had its roots in the Age of Greatness: the Hats seeking security by expansion; the Caps looking back to their spiritual father, Charles XI. And in the lost provinces the memory of the Swedish connexion grew warmer as their subjection to Russia grew more intolerable: in 1788 the Russian government feared, not without reason, that the Estonians might rise to welcome a Swedish return.[2] The Caroline *bussar* long survived their return from Tobolsk, to keep memories alive;[3] and already in the 1720s Charles XII had become (as he still remains) a matter of fierce controversy and bitter partisanship. Not until the latter half of the nineteenth century, when the brief fire of Scandinavianism had burnt itself out, did Sweden adjust herself to her new *rôle* of professional neutral and self-appointed international *censor morum*. Even the cool rationalism of the Age of Liberty could not wholly eradicate the traditions of the seventeenth century. If the last true Rudbeckian was Pehr Tham of Dagsnäs, Rudbeck's weakness for the colossal appears again in Ling's *Asarne* and Fogelberg's statuary; and the foundation of the Gothic League in 1811 gave to Rudbeckianism a fleeting second spring, which produced (as its predecessor had not) a handful of great literature. (And, incidentally, conferred an inestimable boon upon all Swedes by

---

[1] Anna Hamilton Geete, *I solnedgången*, II (Stockholm 1911), p. 306.

[2] Otto Liiv, 'Sverige och Estland under 1700-talet', *Svio-Estonica* 1939, p. 69.

[3] In 1771 A. J. von Höpken could write: 'King Charles's memory was far from being forgotten. The generation which followed him in his campaigns was still to a great extent with us, and devotion to him so strong that he had assuredly been placed among the divinities, if the time when such promotion was the custom could have been brought back': A. J. von Höpken, *Skrifter* (Stockholm 1890), I, p. 256.

reintroducing the antique heroic greeting '*Hej!*', without which Swedish life as we know it would be scarcely conceivable.) But indeed, the Age of Greatness left a deep imprint upon Swedish literature, from Geijer and Tegnér to Topelius and von Heidenstam. And not least upon August Strindberg; who, though he might pillory von Heidenstam in *Svarta fanor* and *Stora landsvägen*, and though he might (at times) hate all that the Age of Greatness stood for, could not escape its fascination: in the majestic series of his historical plays *Gustav Adolf, Kristina* and *Carl XII* bear witness to the unresolved conflict between his aversion and his compassion.[1]

And to-day? What significance, if any, has the imperial experience for the Sweden of Thorbjörn Fälldin and Olof Palme? The visible monuments are certainly better cared for, better appreciated, than a century ago. Nicodemus Tessin, Ehrenstrahl, Krafft, are great names in Sweden's artistic heritage; Anders von Düben's music is heard with some regularity on 6 November; Stiernhielm has his secure place among the great unread classics. The anniversary of Lützen is still celebrated, much as Trafalgar Day is celebrated in England; though perhaps not many Swedes since the time of *Glunten* and *Magister* are conscious that 30 November is 'just Karl den tolftes dag'. And if the classic school of Swedish historiography, from Hallenberg to Ahnlund, no longer holds the field, the military historians, for whom the seventeenth century provides their most satisfying pabulum, have proved surprisingly tenacious of life. *Karolinska Förbundet*, with its annual volume devoted to the period from Charles X to Charles XII, still flourishes, to the great benefit of us all; and the study of the history of the Baltic provinces would be virtually impossible to those of us without the gift of tongues, were it not for the journal *Svio-Estonica*. When all this has been said, however, the Age of Greatness no longer fascinates Swedish historians as once it did; or at least, it no longer fascinates them in the same way. And for the non-historian it can never have the same kind of contemporary relevance as (for instance) the career of Pechlin had for the constitutional controversies of the early twentieth

---

[1] One wonders whether, after all, Strindberg's view of Charles XII may not have been influenced by von Heidenstam, whose essay 'Karl XII och det tragiska' appeared only a year or so earlier than Strindberg's drama.

century. By the man in the street, the lost provinces are simply forgotten. Between the wars the Swedish-speaking coastland of Estonia offered some attraction to tourists, as well as to the specialist in dialects; but those days are gone. Sweden's colonies now lie elsewhere, in the New World: not, indeed, in the sad little enterprise on the Delaware, still less in the inhospitable isle of St Barthélémy, but in the farms and cities of Minnesota and Dakota.

It all happened so long ago; and the efflux of time has allowed the experience to be assimilated, and to be taken for granted. The Swede of to-day, I think, feels neither vainglory nor remorse when confronted with the record: he is happily immune from that unhistorical *mauvaise honte* which troubles our own generation. It may be doubted whether he feels, as he felt even a hundred and fifty years ago, either inspired or reproached by the memories of a heroic past: no

> Hågkomst av de framfarna dagar
> som oss eldar och oss anklagar

finds a place in his intellectual and emotional baggage, as it did in Geijer's. And if in expansive moments he still may be heard alluding to his country as 'Ärans och hjältarnes land', it would be unwise to take him too seriously. But he is conscious too, I think, that the experience of greatness does in some undefined way mark Sweden off from its Scandinavian neighbours; and it may well be that he has some vague intuition that if it had not happened, his country would have been other than it is.